WOMEN
— OF —
THE OLD
TESTAMENT

A Faith of Her Own

J. ELLSWORTH KALAS

Abingdon Press
NASHVILLE

A Faith of Her Own
Women of the Old Testament

Copyright © 2012 by Abingdon Press

All rights reserved.
No part of this work may be reproduced or transmitted in any form or by any means, electronic or mechanical, including photocopying and recording, or by any information storage or retrieval system, except as may be expressly permitted by the 1976 Copyright Act or in writing from the publisher. Requests for permission can be addressed to Permissions, The United Methodist Publishing House, P.O. Box 801, 201 Eighth Avenue South, Nashville, TN 37202-0801, or e-mailed to permissions@umpublishing.org.

This book is printed on acid-free paper.

Library of Congress Cataloging-in-Publication Data

Kalas, J. Ellsworth, 1923–
  A Faith of her own / J. Ellsworth Kalas.
     p.   cm.
ISBN 978-1-4267-4464-8 (book - pbk. / trade pbk. : alk. paper)   1. Women in the Bible.   I. Title.
  BS575.K35   2012
  221.9'22082—dxc23

2012007210

All scripture quotations unless noted otherwise are taken from the New Revised Standard Version of the Bible, copyright © 1989 by the Division of Christian Education of the National Council of the Churches of Christ in the United States of America. Used by permission. All rights reserved.

Scripture quotations noted CEB are from the Common English Bible. Copyright © 2011 by the Common English Bible. All rights reserved. Used by permission. www.CommonEnglishBible.com

Scripture quotations from The Authorized (King James) Version. Rights in the Authorized Version in the United Kingdom are vested in the Crown. Reproduced by permission of the Crown's patentee, Cambridge University Press.

12 13 14 15 16 17 18 19 20 21—10 9 8 7 6 5 4 3 2 1

MANUFACTURED IN THE UNITED STATES OF AMERICA

To all the staff workers at Asbury Theological Seminary who have blessed my life by their daily demonstration of kindness, dedication, efficiency, and love for Christ

Contents

Contents

Foreword

I t is my privilege to introduce to you some of the most fascinating people you will ever know. In many cases their names are already well known to you—for instance, Eve, Sarah, Rachel, Leah, Esther, Ruth. The reason their names are so familiar is because these names started with them, and for several thousand years, people have been naming their daughters after these women. That's reason enough to seek out their stories.

Even though the names have lived on, however, I dare to suggest that most people don't know very much about the remarkable women with whom the names originated. They lived in a world quite different from ours. Thus some might think that there's nothing to be learned from them. True, these women didn't know anything about Facebook, the Internet, television, or radio. Nor did they know about automobiles or airplanes or steamships. They cooked their food over an open fire, carried their garbage to a dump at the village edge, and got their water at the village well.

But there was no need to entertain them with reality shows, because reality was all they knew. Birth and death happened before their eyes and without drugs that might mercifully fog the pain of their experiences. They knew almost everything about life firsthand. Their lessons came raw and untamed and sometimes beautiful and serene. In their world it was more difficult to be superficial because they knew life without camouflage or packaging.

They knew some things about God and faith, especially *a faith of their own*. Like most of us, they learned their most important faith lessons by way of their mistakes and their sins and the sins of other people. The Bible, that most honest of all books, tells their stories with candor and love and sympathy and understanding. And as we read their stories, we know more about who we are and still more about the kind of persons we'd like to become.

I invite you now to meet these women for yourself or to deepen the friendship with them you already enjoy.

—*J. Ellsworth Kalas*

C H A P T E R   O N E

The Ultimate First Lady

Scripture Reading: Genesis 1–4

Some of my favorite friends are people I know only through what they've written. I listen to them with pleasure, sometimes argue with them by notes along the margin of a book, and often laugh with them or nod appreciatively by way of my underlining and bracketing.

Kilian McDonnell, a Benedictine monk and biblical scholar who began writing poetry at age seventy-five, is one such friend. He and I agree on his opinion of several biblical characters (though he doesn't know of my agreeing, more's the pity). Especially, I empathize with his feelings about Eve, that first lady beyond all other first ladies.

Father McDonnell says of Eve that she is smart and confident.[1] Now I must interject, before going further, that while I tend to agree with Father McDonnell, I fear it's also true that it is Eve's confidence and her "muscular . . . intellect" that get her in trouble. But of course trouble is the chance you take when you start thinking. And it's the hazard God took in giving us humans a power that was given to no other creature: the ability to choose between right and wrong. This power is our glory and also our peril. And the First Lady demonstrated as much with a Parisian flair.

Eve had a very special beginning. The Book of Genesis gives it to us in two parts. At first we're told,

> Then God said, "Let us make humankind in our image, according to our likeness; and let them have dominion over the fish of the sea, and over the birds of the air, and over the cattle, and over all the wild animals of the earth, and over every creeping thing that creeps upon the earth."
> So God created humankind in his image,
>   in the image of God he created them;
>   male and female he created them."
> (Genesis 1:26-27)

It is a straightforward but complex, demanding assignment, and it is a team assignment, one that the "male and female" are expected to carry on together. And both of them are created in the image of God.

Then there's a second word, something like a continuing story, as if Genesis were adding details that were left out the first time, or as if the writer wants to give insights that weren't offered in the first account, insights that make some special points. This second report pictures God making the male person first: "then the LORD God formed man from the dust of the ground, and breathed into his nostrils the breath of life; and the man became a living being. And the LORD God planted a garden in Eden, in the east; and there he put the man whom he had formed" (2:7-8). Nothing is said about the woman.

So at this point the man is working a solo operation, and God observes that the man is lonely. God had said during earlier steps in the creation that what was unfolding was "good," but now something is not good. "It is not good that the man should be alone; I will make him a helper as his partner" (2:18). It was soon clear that the partner would have to be very special, a perfect fit, so to speak. Thus, "the LORD God caused a deep sleep to fall upon the man, and he slept; then he took one of his ribs and closed up its place with flesh. And the rib that the LORD God had taken from the man he made into a woman and brought her to the man" (2:21-22). This proved a resounding success. The man said,

> "This at last is bone of my bones
>   And flesh of my flesh;
> this one shall be called Woman,
>   for out of Man this one was taken."

Therefore a man leaves his father and his mother and clings to his wife, and they become one flesh. And the man and his wife were both naked, and were not ashamed. (2:23-25)

Leon R. Kass, medical doctor and bioethicist but especially a student of Genesis, notes that some critics feel that the Genesis account of woman's origin is sexist, indicating dependence on man. He reasons that the scripture supports an opposite view: the man's origin is lower, from the dust, while "the woman begins with the already living flesh and, moreover, from flesh taken close to the heart. Also, the man is, in the process, rendered less than whole. . . . Because he is incomplete and knows it, the man will always be looking for something he lacks."[2]

In any event, the woman's creation is quite an idyllic scene. If you have a touch of sentimentality you might think you hear music playing in the background even as you're reading.

As the Book of Genesis reports, however, it isn't long until the scene turns sour. A villain enters the story, a creature "more crafty than any other wild animal that the LORD God had made" (3:1). Both the man and the woman are present, but the stranger seems to direct his conversation to the woman. She accepts the stranger's proposition, and her husband follows her lead. Father McDonnell sees her as "alley-wise before / the alleys were part of city plans." He has a point!

And Father McDonnell isn't very sympathetic with the man's conduct, saying that it would be odd, indeed, if Adam were to be found blameless in the situation since Eve was made equally from him.[3]

It was on that day that we humans lost our Eden, and I have a feeling—as perhaps you do—that we've been looking for it ever since. And a good many people, including some philosophers and theologians and folks who simply like to speculate lay major blame on the First Lady. Even the apostle Paul belongs to this declaiming group. He writes to the church at Corinth, "But I am afraid that as the serpent deceived Eve by its cunning, your thoughts will be led astray from a sincere and pure devotion to Christ" (2 Corinthians 11:3). A letter to Timothy is more emphatic. "For Adam was formed first, then Eve; and Adam was not deceived, but the woman was deceived and became a transgressor" (1 Timothy 2:13-14).

Frankly, I can't see why Adam was so silent during the conversation between Eve and the serpent. Nor can I excuse him for so readily following Eve's purchase of the forbidden fruit. There's no evidence that he objected at any point. Clearly God charged him with primary responsibility, because when God searched out the transgressing couple he addressed his question to Adam, not Eve: "Have you eaten from the tree of which I commanded you not to eat?" And the man, not to his credit, quickly placed the blame on Eve ("she gave me fruit from the tree") and sought even to project the blame back on God ("The woman whom you gave to be with me") (Genesis 3:11-12). I'd like my ancestor Adam better if he had not been so quick to shunt the blame to others. But even as I say this, I am embarrassed that I have the same tendency to blame others for lapses in my conduct, for my sins, if I may use a true but troublesome word.

I'm not excusing Eve. It's not my business to accuse or excuse her; matters of this sort belong exclusively to God. But I'm impressed by some qualities in Eve, even as I confess that she did wrong. For one, she's an adventuresome soul. Perhaps the serpent saw this quality in her and decided the best way to lead the couple astray was to win Eve's attention. Whether the product is a house, a car, or a refrigerator, a good salesperson gains a foothold by concentrating first on the more persuadable person. In this instance, that person was Eve.

And she was quick of mind. When the serpent misquoted God, Eve quickly set him straight—not realizing that by doing so she was getting into theological waters that would soon be beyond her depth.

And especially, Eve was companionable. She was naturally the first to smile, the first to greet a stranger, the first to make conversation. Of course she was; we know this about her from the very beginning. When the man was alone God saw that he needed "a helper as his partner." Robert Alter, the Hebrew scholar, translates Adam's need for "a sustainer beside him."[4] Begun as a rib from Adam's side, from the place of integrity and embrace, it's the essence of her nature to be companionable.

Lovely as this quality is, it is also the area of Eve's weakness, of her susceptibility. That which is our strength is always also our weakness because, as the dominant part of our person, it is the part most exposed and most frequently left unguarded. We are cautious about our weaknesses (if we know them, that is!), but we are confident in our strengths and therefore not properly attentive to their vulnerabilities. Besides, it's hard to see the vulnerability that is hidden in our strength.

Well, they went wrong, no doubt about it. The man and the woman went wrong. And yes, the woman led the way. But she did so partly because the man retreated. Not only does nature abhor a vacuum, so too does leadership. In truth, I don't think the story would have turned out any differently if Adam had led the conversation with the serpent. But neither does his silence win him some sort of Edenic Nobel prize.

Nevertheless, it's time to say a good word for the man. As the man and woman pick up the pieces of their lives following God's pronouncement of judgment, Adam names his wife. Eve, he says, shall be her name, "because she was the mother of all living" (3:20). If he had been a lesser person, he might have looked upon his wife as the bearer of death. After all, she had led the way in the transgression that brought death upon them and brought their expulsion from the garden. And since he was so quick to transfer blame to his wife when God confronted them for their sin, we wouldn't have been surprised if Adam had found a name for his wife that was at best neutral and at worst condemning. Instead he named her "mother of life." He recognized that the future lay in this remarkable First Lady.

This naming event is a moment of grace and hope. Eden is gone; the gate is locked behind them. Innocence is gone; God has provided them with garments to cover their nakedness. Nature is no longer unanimously on their side; now it will also bring forth "thorns and thistles," and to gain its benefits will mean working by "the sweat of your face" (3:19). Furthermore, when each human life comes to an end, the human will "return to the ground" from which the raw material has been taken. But in the face of all this that is so negative, Adam sees *life*, and he sees it in his companion. Therefore, he reasons, he must name her *life*. And with that, he takes hold of a future of hope, regardless of all the tragedy that at the moment is so dominant. Adam looks at the woman and names her *life*. At this moment in the story, I'm proud to be one of Adam's descendants.

Eve lives up to Adam's faith and more because she has a faith of her own. When God passed judgment on the serpent, the woman, and the man, there was an encouraging word for the woman in the curse pronounced on the serpent.

> "I will put enmity between you and the woman,
>   and between your offspring and hers;
> he will strike your head,
>   and you will strike his heel." (3:15)

There will be continuing conflict between the serpent and the woman's offspring and mutual suffering—but the suffering inflicted on the serpent by the woman's offspring will be much more dramatic than that which the woman's offspring suffers.

It seems clear that Eve remembers this promise when she conceives and bears her first child. She names him *Cain*, which in the Hebrew sounds like "produced" or "gotten." As Robert Alter's translation puts it, "I have got me a man with the Lord." Alter comments, "Eve, upon bringing forth the third human being, imagines herself as a kind of partner of God in man-making."[5] Eve had been told that she would experience pain in childbearing, but her response to this first child is not only a spirit of joy and gratitude but also a sense of divine service. She sees herself as a co-laborer with God.

And in this naming of Cain, Eve also seems to calculate that with this child she will get revenge on the serpent. If this child is, indeed, someone she has gotten with God's help, she can count on him to inflict judgment on the adversary that has robbed them of Eden.

I love Eve's faith and optimism. Unfortunately, the optimism is not well-founded. Instead of carrying forward a new, godly character, Cain reflects the spirit that got Adam and Eve expelled from the Garden. Adam and Eve's sin was, among other things, an attempt to find a quick path to godliness; "you will be like God," the serpent had promised (3:5), but he didn't mention that there are no shortcuts to true godliness. Cain, when grown up, seems susceptible to the same weakness. The writer of Genesis doesn't give us many details. We're told that when Cain and Abel brought their offerings to God, Cain—as a farmer—brought "the fruit of the ground," while Abel—a herdsman—brought "of the firstlings of his flock, their fat portions" (4:3-4). There is a hint that Abel's offering represents specific sacrifice, since he brings a firstling, and the "fat portions," at that. But we learn more about the lack of quality in Cain's worship in that he becomes "very angry" when he realizes that God doesn't approve of his offering. True worship ought not to result in anger. And when we're in trouble we do well to seek the reason rather than becoming upset. God tried to help Cain, urging him to resist the sin that was "lurking" at his door. Instead of responding to God's generous invitation, Cain killed his brother, Abel.

So new tragedy has come into the first family. But with all of this heartbreak, Eve doesn't give up, nor does Adam. With the younger son killed and the older son banished because of his crime, the couple are now essentially childless. So they conceive again, and another son is born. Eve names this one *Seth*, which in the Hebrew sounds like "appointed"—because, Eve says, "God has appointed for me another child instead of Abel, because Cain killed him" (4:25). And it is from Seth's line that "people began to invoke the name of the LORD" (4:26).

Professor Kass sees new maturity in Eve in the birth of this third son. "Seth, unlike Cain, is received as a gift— from beyond, precious, unmerited. Seth, unlike Cain, will be less likely to suffer from excessive parental expectations."[6]

I see Seth as one of the early instances of the grace of God. When the Genesis story shows us humans moving from disobedience in Eden to murder in the family, we might conclude that our story is going to end in hopeless ignominy. Instead, God gives another chance, through the birth of Seth. But when God extends grace, there must be a recipient, a carrier. Grace doesn't hang in the air like a cloud, it works in and through human beings. Eve serves as the receptacle and carrier. She bears the child of grace, and knows the name the child deserves. She knows that the child is an appointed one. The human story will go on. It won't end with the death of goodness in Abel or the spirit of jealousy and murder in Cain. Eve sees an "appointed" quality at work in this new child. Seth is an act of God's grace, and Eve is a knowing partner in the grace enterprise.

Some people read the story of Adam and Eve as a particular story about two specific persons. Others read it as a symbolic story, the saga of our human race, repeated endlessly over the centuries. I feel that neither one gives proper sympathy or credit to Eve. She loses her original home, her husband blames her exclusively for the troubles, and her first child murders her second child. If that isn't enough to make you weep, you have a pretty hard heart.

But the First Lady rises above it. She had named her first child with hope and faith, and when he disappointed her and she lost both of her first sons by the sin of the son of hope, she didn't stop hoping. She conceived again, and believed again, and once more expressed her faith in the name she gave to this third child. And in it all, she saw herself in partnership with God in her role of transmitting life. It's true that she got in trouble by her brash conversation with the tempter, but her disastrous misstep didn't make her give up on theology or on God. I like to think that the best of Eve is coming through when I read that after the birth of her grandson, Enosh, "people began to invoke the name of the Lord" (4:26). With all her problems, Eve proved with her faith, her courage, and her resiliency to be a most remarkable First Lady.

CHAPTER TWO

A Woman Who Married Trouble

Scripture Reading: Genesis 4:1-17

Where did Cain get his wife? In the world of my childhood this was a favorite question for those who wanted to question biblical accuracy. Genesis tells its story in quite sparse fashion, reporting that Adam and Eve had two sons, Cain and Abel, and that after Cain killed his brother, they had another son whom they named Seth. But nothing was said about women other than Eve until the writer of Genesis reports, "Cain knew his wife, and she conceived and bore Enoch" (Genesis 4:17). Where did she come from, this anonymous person who carried on the line of the first infamous biblical personality?

I remember a long-ago evangelist who posed the question rhetorically, then answered, "Cain got his wife where every man gets his wife: from his mother-in-law." The audience laughed appreciatively and resolved they would pass the story to their neighbor the next day. But of course the evangelist's humor did nothing to answer the question. And in a sense, it's just as well.

In truth, Bible readers of a variety of religious convictions seem more concerned about this detail than was the author of the Book of Genesis. He tells us the tragic story of an older brother, Cain, who became jealous of his younger brother, Abel. God urged Cain to repent of his attitude (after all, it is from our attitudes that our conduct eventually takes shape), but Cain chose instead to kill his brother. After God confronted Cain with his crime, Genesis reports simply, "Then Cain went away from the presence of the LORD, and settled in the land of Nod, east of Eden. Cain knew his wife, and she conceived and bore Enoch" (Genesis 4:16-17a).

Thus the writer of Genesis leaves questions unanswered for us. Were there other humans besides Adam and Eve and their descendants, who lived in this "land of Nod, east of Eden"? Or did Adam and Eve have a number of children besides those that are mentioned, including daughters? And did Cain marry one of his sisters? Genesis seems not the least concerned about this question. Why not? Because as the story of Genesis unfolds, the crucial point of the story is the issue of good and evil in all of its pain and complexity and wonder, not the origins of all humans involved. I dare to suggest that those who raise the issue of the Bible's accuracy by way of Cain's wife and those who work to defend it are both wasting their time and missing the point. If the writer of Genesis could speak to us, I think he might say, "Get on with the story, before you miss the point."

I'm not going far into Cain's story in examining the greater story of our human race. I want only to think with you for a while about the anonymous woman who bore children to Cain. Whether she was his sister or whether she was an inhabitant of the land of Nod, I do not know, and as I have already indicated, I don't really care. If I were simply a student of literature, I would know that this is a remarkable story and I would conclude that the storyteller felt the source of Cain's wife was no issue to the plot. As it happens, I see the biblical story as uniquely inspired of God, and this leads me to basically the same conclusion: Mrs. Cain's origin is incidental to the story.

But human beings fascinate me. This is why I love literature in general and the Bible in particular. I wonder what makes us tick and why we do the things we do. This is no idle curiosity on my part. It is essential to my calling. I began to preach as a teenager, and at total, preachers need to acquaint themselves with two persons: God and their fellow humans. I realized early that I must understand humans if I were to preach to them, especially as humans make the choices that shape their lives for time and eternity.

In a sense this brings me back to the question with which we began this chapter: where did Cain get his wife? But as I ask it, the question has a human, psychological bent: where in the world was there a woman who would want to marry a fellow like Cain? Why would someone want to marry trouble?

As it happens, the Bible doesn't tell us when Cain and his wife married. We read that after Cain murdered his brother, he "settled in the land of Nod, east of Eden. Cain knew his wife, and she conceived and bore Enoch" (Genesis 4:16b-17a). This sequence makes it appear that the marriage took place after Cain had fled his homeland for Nod. The great fourth-century scholar, Ephrem the Syrian, said that Cain "separated himself from his parents and his kin because he saw that they would not intermarry with him."[1] This is speculation, but it's reasonable.

But I submit that even if Cain and his wife-to-be had grown up in some proximity, giving them a chance to observe each other over a period of time, the woman surely ought to have seen signs of trouble. Cain was the apple of his mother's eye. As we noted in our study of Eve, she saw herself in partnership with God in the birth of Cain, and she named him accordingly. Obviously it's no crime to be wanted and greatly loved; every child should be blessed with such a reception. But if the birth expectations are unreasonable, the high compliment can become an unbearable burden. Then along came Cain's little brother, Abel— hardly more than an afterthought, it would seem, but competition, nevertheless. Now there were two to share the devotion of Adam and Eve, and Cain no doubt saw the decimation of his inherent privileges.

This scenario is as common as the human race. Nevertheless, it has inevitable problems. When they work out well, the siblings are both better for it, but when there is mishandling or when some of the differences are toxic, almost anything can happen.

Once grown, the two men followed different career paths, with Cain a farmer and Abel a herdsman. We moderns may classify the two jobs under the broad category of "agriculture," but there seems always to have been a built-in antagonism in the two cultures. Nevertheless, their work could have been complementary rather than competitive if it hadn't been for what happened on the day when they chose to worship God with their thank offerings. Cain resented God's response to their respective offerings, because it was clear that God approved of Abel's gifts while disapproving of Cain's.

Was Cain so accustomed to being the favored one that he couldn't handle second place? If so, he was not going to be easy to live with. Life requires all of us to take second place at times. Marriage requires that each partner be able at appropriate times to take second place; and it is often in second place that our true character has a chance to grow. This is especially true if we've been accustomed to the champion's seat.

What worries me most about Cain's personality is his unwillingness to repent. We humans err. We've been doing so since Adam and Eve. Sometimes our sins are grievous and intentional. More often they result from poor thinking and spiritual dullness, the kind of attitude that gets us in trouble before we realize how badly we're off track. But God in mercy allows us to start again. Nowhere is this so clear as in Cain's story. When he is so angry that his countenance falls, God patiently pursues him, warning him that he is on the way to trouble and telling him how he can change his ways. God assures him that he can "master" the evil lurking in his soul.

But instead of repenting of his feelings of jealousy, Cain gave them full rein. His act of violence did not come from a moment of lost control; to the contrary, he planned each detail, with the evil genius of a bitter soul. He invited Abel to go out into the field. The biblical word implies a place away from human habitation, among the wild beasts. There Cain killed his brother. Nor did any remorse follow the crime. When God asked, "Where is your brother Abel," Cain answered, "I do not know; am I my brother's keeper?" (Genesis 4:9). Father Paul Mankowski points out that Cain used the term in such a way as to say essentially, "Am I the shepherd's shepherd?" thus showing his contempt for his brother's occupation.[2]

I am trying to help you and me see the kind of person Cain was. I confess that I'm painting a dark picture. It's difficult, however, to see redeeming elements. When God tells Cain that the ground will no longer yield its strength to his efforts and that he will be "a fugitive and a wanderer on the earth," Cain still speaks no word of regret or repentance: "My punishment is greater than I can bear!" (Genesis 4:13). He says that God has driven him away from the soil, not acknowledging that this alienation is a result of his own conduct, nor does he remember that God had forewarned him. He fears now that anyone who meets him may kill him, reflecting our human tendency to judge others by the flaws in our own character. Worst of all, he makes no effort to restore his relationship with God. The writer of Genesis puts it with eloquent simplicity: "Then Cain went away from the presence of the LORD" (Genesis 4:16). God didn't move away from Cain; Cain moved away from God. If we humans get away from the presence of the LORD, it is by a closure in our souls, because as the psalmist later writes so powerfully, there is no place where we can flee from God's presence (Psalm 139). Cain "settled in the land of Nod" (Genesis 4:16), literally meaning the land of "wandering." He made wandering his habitation. A poet might say that Cain was a restless soul.

But then a woman came into Cain's life. As I said earlier, we don't know when he married, nor do we know whether she was from his home area or from Nod. We only know that now Cain "knew" her—the highly insightful biblical word for sexual union. Why did this woman marry Cain? You may be ready to offer any number of answers. The marital market was small. Or, it was a man's world and women married as their fathers or older brothers dictated. Or, she fell in love and love is blind. Or (a cynical voice), the woman wasn't very sharp.

You could be right in any of these judgments. But from what I've seen of women in a lifetime as pastor, preacher, teacher, and student of human nature, I offer another explanation. Perhaps she was a victim of unbridled idealism: she thought she could help Cain become a better man. At our best (and sometimes at our most naive), we all have such dreams. I think women have the dream more often than men do, however.

When I was a seminary student a professor greeted us one day with a gentle form of humor popular at the time, "Confucius say." "Confucius say, 'Many a woman marry a man to mend his ways. Find out he's not worth a darn.'" I tried the line with my class recently and discovered that only the two students past forty-five years of age got the joke since they were the only persons who knew that *darn* is defined as "to mend, as torn clothing, with rows of stitches."

But even if the play on words is lost, the principle remains. Women have an extraordinary gift for believing that they can redeem a lost cause. My memory brings up a montage of women's faces, especially in their late teens or twenties, speaking essentially the same line: "My parents [counselors, friends, etc.] tell me that I shouldn't go with him, but I believe he can change. I know he's been in a lot of trouble, but he can change. I just know he can. I think my love can make the difference." It's the fairy tale of the princess who kisses a frog and he becomes a prince. We love such stories, and we want them to come true.

Sometimes, however, it is as the poet-playwright Lionel Wiggam put it, a "Grim Fairy Tale." The princess kisses her frog, but the frog doesn't change. Instead, as the poem ends, he has "turned the princess into a frog."[3] That's the other montage in my memory, this one of women in midlife or later whose anticipated fairy tale turns out quite another way.

But I refuse to be a pessimist. I keep hoping for our human race and its individual parts. I keep hoping for the woman who married Cain, and I have two pieces of hopeful evidence. John Chrysostom, Bishop of Constantinople in the late fourth century and one of the great preachers of the ages, reasoned that God's punishment of Cain was not to make him suffer but to reform him. "God let him live a long time with that bodily tremor of his. . . . It served to teach all men and exhort them never to dare do what he

21

had done, so that they might not suffer the same punishment. And Cain himself became a better man again."[4]

Was the venerable Chrysostom right? Did Cain become a better man again? I don't know, and there is no strong substantive proof. I am intrigued by what happened when Cain's son, Enoch, was born. We read that after Enoch's birth, Cain "built a city, and named it Enoch after his son Enoch" (Genesis 4:17b). I have interpreted this sentence both positively and negatively, as either an act of defiance against God's judgment of "fugitive and wanderer" upon Cain (4:12) or as a symbol of redemption, that Cain was starting life anew through his son.

But at the least, I see Cain demonstrating classical parental love, as he seeks to make a better life for Enoch than he himself had known. Cain's path was that of a fugitive, with no sure dwelling place. He built a city for his son, and to be sure that his son would not be a fugitive, he put the boy's name on the city.

I am an optimist for a second reason. It's an anecdotal one to be sure, but if one can accumulate enough anecdotal evidence one has the stuff that makes a statistical study of sorts. I'm thinking at this moment of a friend who, if he were still living, would probably authorize me to use his name. He spoke often, gratefully and proudly, of the difference his wife had made in his life. He said that without her he would have remained the resentful, rebellious young man he was when he finished high school. Instead, he became an admirable Christian, known widely for his readiness always to assist those who needed help of one kind or another. His wife kissed a potential rebel and made him a prince.

Now if this were the only case of its kind, I would hesitate to mention it. But as you know, it is one of many. You've been in many conversations that included the sentence, "You can't help wondering what would have happened to (you supply the name) if he hadn't married the person he did."

Believe me, I'm not making a blanket case for marrying Cain. If I'm around when my granddaughters reach the marrying age, I will no doubt want to counsel them against unreasonable idealism. And yet, what would happen to vast numbers of persons, male and female, if it were not for those idealists who see something in them that society as a whole does not recognize? What chance is there for the Cains of this world if someone doesn't think that they're worth a redemptive kiss?

I know what you may be thinking, and perhaps you're right. The woman who married Cain may have been an inhabitant of Nod who didn't know Cain's history. Or she may have been party to an arranged marriage, with no choice on her part. And we don't know, beyond the speculative evidence I've given, if Cain ever turned out right, though I like to cast my vote with Chrysostom.

Nevertheless, I decided in the end to include this anonymous woman, Cain's wife, in the list of those with "a faith of her own." I do so in honor of a peculiar idealism that women seem often to have in larger than reasonable supply. I weep for those—whether son, brother, friend, or spouse—who remain a frog. But blessed be God, it is beautiful when the idealism produces a prince.

CHAPTER THREE

The Compleat Woman

Scripture Reading: Genesis 11:27-30, 12:1-5a

Your dictionary will tell you that my spelling of *complete* is archaic. In a sense, that's why I've chosen to use it. Not because I think women like Sarah, the subject of this chapter, no longer exist; to the contrary, this book comes from the conviction that the best characteristics of these Old Testament women are in abundant display in our twenty-first-century world. I have chosen the archaic spelling because it helps me underline the thoroughly

remarkable person we have in this woman named
Sarah.

When the Book of Genesis introduces Sarah, however,
the writer seems intent on letting us know that Sarah was
anything but complete. The sentence of introduction makes
a point of it: "Now Sarai was barren; she had no child"
(Genesis 11:30). In Sarah's world, the culture judged a
woman by her ability to bear children and, more specifically, to bear a son. Children in general and sons in particular meant economic security when parents reached old age.
Also, most of the Old Testament writers saw children as the
only real form of immortality. There are instances where
the Old Testament seems to envision life beyond the grave,
but on the whole the basic hope was that persons would
live on by way of their children.

The writer of Genesis wants us to understand beyond
doubt that Sarah was incomplete in this most basic of func-
tions. He declares the fact twice by stating it ("Now Sarai
was barren") and then underlining it ("she had no child").
With that repetitive statement the writer was also making a
more specific point by answering a question that he knew
would be in the mind of his reader or listener. In that world
and time, if a woman of privilege seemed unable to conceive, it was legal for her personal maid to mate with her
husband, with the understanding that the child that came
from the union would be considered the child of the wife.
Thus the writer is saying not only that Sarah was barren

but also that she and Abraham had chosen not to exercise the option of surrogate motherhood by way of Sarah's maid.

That Abraham and Sarah had not resorted to the common practice of surrogacy tells us several things about them. For one, they had minds of their own. Their culture believed heirs should be gotten at any cost. Abraham and Sarah were not captive to that cultural assumption. Also, we have an indication that Sarah was a strong and compelling woman. If Abraham ever gave thought to the surrogate arrangement, he gave up out of respect for Sarah's opinion or because of the singular quality of his love for her.

Professor Leon R. Kass insists that proper marriage is "an essential element in promoting justice and holiness," then continues,

> Proper marriage and proper patriarchy are hardly the natural ways of humankind. They have to be learned—to begin with, somewhat against the grain. Both require fidelity, not only to spouses and children, but also to the higher moral and spiritual possibilities to which human beings are called.

Dr. Kass notes that Sarah, Rebekah, Leah, and Rachel were all "strong women."[1] I submit that Sarah led the way. When Genesis tells us later, at the time of the marriage of Isaac, son of Abraham and Sarah, that he took his bride, Rebekah, "into his mother Sarah's tent, and he loved her," it isn't hard to see that the writer is making a point. And if there is any doubt, the writer clears it away when he adds, "So Isaac was comforted after his mother's death" (Genesis 24:67). He was finding in Rebekah the strong love that he had known in his mother Sarah and had lost in her death. Nor is it surprising that Isaac and Rebekah's son, Jacob, found the same kind of strength in his wives, Leah and Rachel. Sarah began a pattern of persuasive strength that carried through the stories of the biblical patriarchs, Abraham, Isaac, and Jacob.

I consider Sarah a leader in the truest sense of the word. Specifically, she was an *influencer*, and in the end what is a leader if not an influencer? When we read history with reasonable care we find that sometimes the person in the executive suite or the king's palace was more a figure-head than a leader; the leader was the person influencing the figurehead. I sense that history has had some personalities who found their fulfillment in the pomp and circumstance of their position. Influencers, by contrast, got their satisfaction in knowing that they were bringing particular purposes to pass, even if no one (or few) knew of the influencer's role.

While I am on the subject, let me extend my definition of leadership to the world of teaching and parenting. A good teacher is almost surely a leader, but the leadership shows itself a generation later, through one or many students. A good parent is the quintessential leader, and a wise son or daughter comes later to declare it. Often it is clear that the parent was by usual judgments a relatively obscure person with little or no public acclaim, but an influencer.

When I concur with Professor Kass's description of Sarah, Rebekah, Leah, and Rachel as "strong women," I see them specifically as *influencers*, leaders in their own right. Sometimes, as with Rebekah, they may have been manipulators, sometimes they may have argued a case, and sometimes they may simply have held on doggedly until their position became the established one. But they knew how to lead.

If one is to know how to lead one must also know how to follow. I question the qualifications of any presumed leader who has not shown the ability to follow. A historian could prove what I'm saying by pointing to some kings in the days of royal rule. In that system young men came to the throne and its power without ever having been submissive to anyone, perhaps not even to a preoccupied parent. The same issue operates in the corporate world, small or large. A wise parent insists on the heir-apparent working their way from warehouse to boardroom, but sometimes the son or daughter knows no such experience in following and, as a result, is unprepared for leading.

Sarah knew how to follow. Genesis introduces her to us in the closing verses of chapter 11, then doesn't mention her name in the life-changing opening verses of chapter 12 when God calls Abraham to leave country, kindred, and family heritage to go "to the land that I will show you"

(Genesis 12:1). Sarah isn't mentioned until verse 5: "Abram took his wife Sarai and his brother's son Lot. . . . And they set forth to go to the land of Canaan" (Genesis 12:5). If Sarah expressed any opinions about this life-upsetting journey, we have no record of it.

As I have indicated in both writing and sermons, I have great regard for those persons who operate by secondhand faith. I'm thinking of people like Sarah, who venture with God on the basis of what someone else has heard from God. As a United Methodist minister I became pastor of several churches primarily on the judgment of my bishop and his cabinet. I came to agree with the counsel, but by second hand. I support a number of missionary causes because I believe in the persons who lead them (often my former students) and in the conviction they have that God has called them to such a work. They are Abraham and I am Sarah.

Twice Sarah followed Abraham when I think she would have been justified in arguing the case. There's no evidence, however, that she did so. There came a time in Abraham and Sarah's journey when there was a famine in the land. They were running a good-sized agribusiness, with a large number of employees and hundreds if not thousands of cattle, sheep, and goats, moving to find pastureland in unsettled, unclaimed country. There was one solution to famine in the ancient Middle East: go to Egypt, where the Nile River always carried the hope of fruitfulness.

Abraham was an exemplar of faith, but at this point, he faltered:

> "I know well that you are a woman beautiful in appearance," he told Sarah, "and when the Egyptians see you, they will say, 'This is his wife'; then they will kill me, but they will let you live. Say you are my sister, so that it may go well with me because of you, and that my life may be spared on your account." (Genesis 12:11-13)

As you and I read this story, Abraham seems coldly pragmatic. He isn't lying; Sarah is in fact his half-sister. But neither is he telling the whole truth. Also, he is putting Sarah in a situation where she will almost surely be treated as a prostitute. His logic seems to be that unless he does so, he will be killed and she will become the sexual property of the Egyptians. I don't approve of Abraham's act, but neither do I pass judgment on it. Judgment is God's business, not mine, and I try increasingly to remember this fact.

Genesis reports the story matter-of-factly but without salacious adornment. The Egyptians do, indeed, find Sarah attractive. Apparently they see in her a kind of regal bearing that persuades them that Pharaoh would find her attractive too. He takes her as "my wife" (12:19). But God sends affliction on Pharaoh and his household, and Pharaoh sends Abraham and Sarah and all of their household on their way with a vigorous admonition. Abraham resorted to the same ruse years later at Gerar. This time God spared King Abimelech by a warning dream. If it seems that Sarah is quite old to be so attractive, I suggest that Genesis is saying not only that beauty and sensuality can be quite timeless but also that Sarah was a very beautiful, very remarkable woman, the kind that a modern writer might call "enchanting."

Yet with all life's other favors, Sarah was still unable to conceive. When God called Abraham (Genesis 12:1-3) it was with the promise that he would become "a great nation." For this to happen, Abraham and Sarah must have children. Sarah assumes that the fault is hers, and she now turns to a solution she and Abraham had not employed in earlier years; she instructs Abraham to cohabit with her Egyptian slave girl, Hagar. Hagar conceives and very quickly the relationship between Sarah and Hagar turns bitter. Probably a novelist would tell us that a woman of Sarah's beauty and strength will bear no rival. Hagar runs away but returns under God's direction, and eventually a son, Ishmael, is born.

Some thirteen years pass by. By this time Abraham is satisfied that Ishmael is the one through whom God will fulfill the promise of "a great nation." When God says that Sarah will conceive, Abraham contests the point: "O that Ishmael might live in your sight!" (Genesis 17:18). And when Sarah hears that she would still conceive after "it had ceased to be with [her] after the manner of women," she "laughed to herself" (Genesis 18:11-12).

So at age ninety, Sarah became a mother. She named the child Isaac, which means "laughter." It was a name of joy, no doubt about that, but perhaps it also reflected ironic humor that she had laughed when hearing that she would become a mother and that such a thing could happen at her time of life. But Isaac was more than laughter.

With an older half-brother whom his father had previously seen as a satisfactory heir, his place seemed to his mother to be open to contention. During a festive celebration on the day of Isaac's weaning, Sarah saw something that upset her. "So she said to Abraham, 'Cast out this slave woman with her son; for the son of this slave woman shall not inherit along with my son Isaac'" (Genesis 21:10).

It was not Sarah's finest hour. She robs Hagar of the identity of her name, referring to her twice as "this slave woman." Ishmael, whom Sarah had originally planned to claim as her legal son, is now "*her* son," while Isaac is "*my* son." The language is all true, but it is also mean and vengeful—a reminder that we can speak the truth but use it as a weapon. In it all, Sarah is paying for the time fourteen years earlier when she took matters into her own hands. Sarah, as we have said, was a strong woman—a very strong woman—but the price of strength is sometimes its penalty.

From the point of view of the biblical story, however, Sarah has done what is right. The Book of Genesis makes clear that the line of descent is to be through Abraham and Sarah. Abraham, out of love and sentiment, may waver on this matter, but not Sarah. In a sense she believes in God's promise to Abraham more resolutely than does Abraham himself.

We do not read of Sarah again until we read the notice of her death. It is especially significant that Sarah is not mentioned in the climactic event in Isaac's late boyhood or early manhood, when he and his father go to the place of Abraham's ultimate trial of faith, the possible sacrifice of Isaac. In brief, Genesis tells us, "After these things God tested Abraham" (22:1). The test was that Abraham was to take his son, his "only son Isaac, whom you love" (22:2) to a place some distance away where he would offer him to God as a burnt sacrifice. At the last moment, God intervened and Isaac's life was spared.

The dramatic incident never mentions Sarah. This is more than incidental considering the partnership she and Abraham had enjoyed for a long lifetime together. It is still more significant in light of the special relationship Sarah had with her son, which I indicated earlier and to which I shall give more attention shortly. Did Abraham not tell Sarah what he was doing out of respect for her feelings—or more likely out of fear for her reaction? Or did Abraham consider this terrifying assignment something exclusively between him and God, something so singular that he could not discuss it with anyone? Whatever the reason, Sarah, who had journeyed with Abraham from Ur to Haran to the unknown Canaan, to Egypt and Gerar, who had experienced with him years of frustration and disappointment and no doubt many vigorous discussions, is not with him on this three-day trek into the wilderness, a journey more important to her than everything else that has happened in her long lifetime.

If Sarah knew what was happening, without of course knowing its eventual outcome, it had to be the longest week of her life, a personal Armageddon packed into a half dozen days. If she did not know what was happening, I can't help believing that her maternal and marital instincts told her something was exceedingly out of joint. In either scenario, these days were a capstone to Sarah's life and to her walk with God. When the writer of Genesis tells us that "God tested Abraham," I wonder how he dared to leave out Sarah, unless we are meant to infer that she didn't know.

Perhaps the answer comes in a sentence of unique tribute several years after Sarah's death. After Abraham and Isaac's trip to Mount Moriah, the writer tells us simply that they went to Beersheba together and that Abraham lived there. Then, after a report on births and marriages among Abraham's kin back in Haran—including the first mention of Rebekah, who will soon be a key figure in the story—Genesis says, "Sarah lived for one hundred twenty-seven years; this was the length of Sarah's life" (23:1). It goes on to report Abraham's mourning and the rather detailed negotiations that were necessary in his purchasing a burial place for Sarah.

Some three years after Sarah's death, Abraham sent his most trusted servant back to his homeland to find a wife for Isaac. The servant, worthy of the trust and himself a man of faith, brought back Rebekah. Isaac was now making his home in the Negeb. It is evening, and Isaac "went out . . . to walk in the field" (Genesis 24:63)—the kind of scene that has inspired romantic songwriters for untold centuries. The servant introduced Rebekah to Isaac with the story of his journey. "Then Isaac brought her into his mother Sarah's tent. He took Rebekah, and she became his wife; and he loved her. So Isaac was comforted after his mother's death" (Genesis 24:67).

Our psychology-fascinated age may have its own interpretation of Isaac's taking his bride into his mother's tent. I submit that the act is a tribute to both women. It may be, as many scholars say, that Isaac was always somewhat estranged from his father after the Moriah incident. In any event, his mother was his full-orbed defender. Abraham may have had two sons, but Sarah had only one, and she poured her soul into him. For Isaac to place Rebekah in Sarah's tent was the ultimate tribute. She was now the primary person in his life. For three years he had grieved his mother's loss. Now he was "comforted." To be more specific, "he loved her [Rebekah]."

Sarah was not perfect, but she was compleat. And there's nothing archaic about that.

CHAPTER FOUR

A Mother Who Played Favorites

Scripture Reading: Genesis 25:19-28

My title puts the woman Rebekah at a disadvantage. Parents in general and mothers in particular are supposed to love their children equally and to treat them with circumspect fairness. If a parent senses a prejudice for one child over another, she usually leans hard the other way to correct the perceived injustice. Not so with Rebekah. The mother of twins, she favored one over the other and she invested her considerable skills in making her favoritism

count. In time it appears that she paid dearly for what she
did. Nevertheless, I am casting a solid vote for Rebekah. I
do not approve of all that she did (not that my opinion
matters to her or to anyone else), but I admire the insight
and perception that motivated her conduct.

Rebekah enters the biblical story by influences both
human and divine. God had started something unique in
calling Abraham. Through him, God said, "all the families
of the earth shall be blessed" (Genesis 12:3). Abraham's son
Isaac becomes the carrier of that blessing, and thus much
depends on the person Isaac marries. But no woman except
his mother appears in Isaac's life, so when Isaac is forty
years old, Abraham sends his trusted servant to get a wife
for his son. Although Canaan is to be the geographical
home for Abraham and his descendants, it is not their spiritual base. Abraham therefore sends the servant back to his
own people. It is with the assurance that God "would send
his angel" (24:7) before him.

The servant believed Abraham so fully that when
he neared his destination at a well—the community
meeting place in that ancient world—he made a specific
request:

> Let the girl to whom I shall say, "Please offer your jar that I
> may drink," and who shall say, "Drink, and I will water
> your camels"—let her be the one whom you have appointed
> for your servant Isaac. By this I shall know that you have
> shown steadfast love to my master. (Genesis 24:14)

It was quite a prayer. Professor Kass reminds us that a typical camel will drink twenty-five gallons of water when dehydrated. It wasn't a matter of turning on a spigot; one had to draw the water from a well, then pour it into a trough. In truth, the servant was asking for a miracle-sign that was also a sublime evidence of character. But while he was still praying, "there was Rebekah, who was born to Bethuel son of Milcah, the wife of Nahor, Abraham's brother, coming out with her water-jar on her shoulder" (24:15). And in case you are wondering, "The girl was very fair to look upon, a virgin whom no man had known" (24:16). When the servant asked the young woman the test question, "Please let me sip a little water from your jar," the young woman answered, "Drink, my lord." Then, "I will draw water for your camels also, until they have finished drinking" (24:17-19).

The servant had the answer to his prayer. This was the divine portion of the story. But a human issue remained. How would the girl's family respond when a stranger appeared with his story about seeking a wife for his master's son? Rebekah's brother, Laban (of whom we will hear more later) was the main spokesperson in the young girl's household. When Rebekah returned with the stranger, Laban immediately noticed the gold nose ring and the gold bracelets the stranger had given her. Obviously this put Laban in a receptive mood. This is the human side of the story; this and the knowledge that the prospective bridegroom was the son of their uncle Abraham. The next day Rebekah was on her way to meet the man with whom she would spend the rest of her life.

It isn't your twenty-first-century love story, and in most respects, Rebekah isn't your twenty-first-century girl. It's hard to imagine a young woman toting water for the animals at a village well, but it was standard for that day and culture. Nor can we imagine a woman's choice of husband being decided by her parents and her older brother: in this case, particularly her older brother. But this, too, was the way of the time. And for that matter, neither do we expect a father to send one of his executive assistants to find a wife for his son. Our century's plotline says, "Fall in love, then marry." The story of Isaac and Rebekah and of most of the people of their world lived by the rule, "Marry according to the plans laid out by your parents, then learn to love each other."

We know several things already about Rebekah. She was, as we have noted, "very fair to look upon," and a virgin. She was young, probably in her mid-teens; the Bible calls her a *girl.* Isaac was a man of forty, probably a quarter of a century older. Rebekah was industrious. When the servant asked her for a drink, she "*quickly* lowered her jar," and when she offered to water the camels again she "*quickly* emptied her jar into the trough and *ran* again to the well to draw" (24:18, 20; italics added). The Bible says that while she was doing all of this, Abraham's servant "gazed at her in silence" (24:21). If I had been there I would have gazed in amazement.

And she was a decisive person. When Abraham's servant explained his mission to Rebekah's father and brother, they quickly agreed. "Look, Rebekah is before you; take her and go, and let her be the wife of your master's son" (24:51). So the next morning Abraham's servant was ready to return, mission accomplished. Rebekah's mother and brother answered, "Let the girl remain with us a while, at least ten days; after that she may go" (24:55). It was in every way a reasonable request, but the servant was in a hurry. At this point they sought Rebekah's opinion (a little late, it seems to a modern reader): "Will you go with this man?" Rebekah's answer was to the point: "I will" (24:58). There were no wasted words, no lengthy speech, no dramatic pause, no hesitation for effect. There is no hint that she had to give the matter further consideration. She knew what she wanted, or perhaps more important, what she considered right. "Rebekah and her maids rose up and mounted the camels, and followed the man" (24:61).

Genesis tells us that Isaac loved his wife and that in her he found comfort in the loss of his mother, but it doesn't tell us whether Rebekah loved Isaac in return. If anyone had asked Rebekah, she might have answered as did Tevye's wife in the musical, *Fiddler on the Roof,* by reciting all she was doing for him. I think Rebekah evoked a tenderness in Isaac that made him sensitive to her needs. Genesis does not tell us as much about Isaac's personal relationship to God as it does about his father, Abraham, or his son Jacob, but there is this significant word: "Isaac prayed to the LORD for his wife, because she was barren; and the LORD granted his prayer, and his wife Rebekah conceived" (25:21).

The pregnancy was not pleasant. "The children struggled together within her," (25:22) and not knowing that she was carrying twins, Rebekah only knew that her days were increasingly miserable. When she cried out to God she received more of an answer than she could have anticipated. First, that there were "two nations" in her womb— mind you, not simply two children, but the beginning of two political entities, a history in embryo—and that "the elder shall serve the younger" (25:23).

The idea of the elder serving the younger was out of all proper order for the ancient world, and indeed for most of the world today, including probably a majority of the world's laws. Only a very strong and very self-assured person could handle such a message. It is not incidental that the message came to Rebekah rather than to Isaac. I am not disparaging Isaac; I sympathize with him in many ways. But I venture that Isaac was more compliant with the mores of his world and that he would have found it very difficult to cooperate in violating those standards. God trusted the divine plan to Rebekah.

This is why I dare to describe Rebekah as "a mother who played favorites." I don't see her as someone who operated from petty prejudices, nor do I feel that she neglected Esau to Jacob's advantage. Nevertheless, I'm sure that as she watched the boys grow up she kept a sensitive eye on Jacob. There was something special about this child; he had a heightened role in God's plan, and it was her duty to shepherd that role to fulfillment.

The twins' natural proclivities made it easy for her. At birth Esau "came out red, all his body like a hairy mantle," and Jacob emerged "with his hand gripping Esau's heel" (25:25-26), as if he were already striving for the supremacy God has promised for him. "When the boys grew up, Esau was a skillful hunter, a man of the field, while Jacob was a quiet man, living in tents. Isaac loved Esau, because he was fond of game; but Rebekah loved Jacob" (25:27-28). Genesis tells us why Isaac loved Esau, and it strikes us as a very sensual, materialistic reason. Mind you, it is not that Isaac loved to go hunting with Esau but simply that he loved the game Esau brought home. Genesis doesn't tell us why Rebekah loved Jacob. A reader may justifiably judge that it is because he was a homebody, "living in tents," and of course this must have been a normal, human factor in Rebekah's love for Jacob. But the plotline is deeper. Rebekah knows that this boy is special. A unique future lies with him. God told her so when she was in the throes of a difficult pregnancy.

You no doubt know the story of a showdown between the two young men. Even if you're not familiar with much

of the Bible you probably know how one evening Esau
came home from an unsuccessful hunting expedition. When
he caught the fragrance of the soup Jacob was cooking, he
asked for a serving. Jacob said a ridiculous thing: "I'll give
you a bowl of soup for your birthright." If Esau had been a
better man he would have said, "You have to be kidding."
Instead Esau reasoned that if he didn't get something to eat
he would die (which shows us something of the way Esau
dealt with life), and he traded his birthright for a bowl of
soup (27:31-32).

I don't know if Jacob ever confided in his mother about
this event, but she played a key role in what happened next,
probably several years later. The boys' father, Isaac, was
now blind and seemed to have given up on life. He felt he
was going to die soon and he wanted one more favorite
meal before he died. As it turned out Isaac lived many years
more; in fact, it appears that he outlived his much younger
wife, Rebekah. But in his hunger for a special meal he
asked his son Esau to bring in a venison, "and bring it to
me to eat, so that I may bless you before I die" (27:4).

Rebekah overheard the conversation. Quickly, she
called in Jacob, told him to get "two choice kids" from the
flock so she could prepare a meal for Jacob to present to
his father—his blind father—and receive his brother Esau's
blessing. Jacob objected because of the dangers involved,
but his mother told him how to complete the act of deception. And that day Isaac's wife and his younger son

deceived him, and he gave to Jacob the blessing that belonged to Esau.

When Esau discovered what had been done, he "said to himself, 'The days of mourning for my father are approaching; then I will kill my brother Jacob'" (27:41). But apparently Esau expressed his anger to some servant because the word was passed on to Rebekah. She warned Jacob:

> Your brother Esau is consoling himself by planning to kill you. Now therefore, my son, obey my voice; flee at once to my brother Laban in Haran, and stay with him a while until your brother's anger turns away . . . and he forgets what you have done to him; then I will send and bring you back from there. Why should I lose both of you in one day? (27:42-45)

Rebekah was both a realist and an optimist, which is a pretty good combination if you can pull it off. She was a realist in recognizing that by joining Jacob in deceiving Isaac she would surely lose most of the loyalties of her son Esau. Esau could hardly have set his mind on killing Jacob and have maintained cordial feelings toward his mother. I don't think he hated her, but the sense of sonship was seriously damaged. However, if Esau killed Jacob, he would become a fugitive and thus both sons would be lost. By sending Jacob away, Rebekah was hoping to have Jacob back after Esau's anger had diminished. Unfortunately, Rebekah was unduly optimistic in thinking that Jacob's absence would be for just "a while." There is no evidence that she ever saw her favorite son again.

A remarkable Jewish scholar, Leon R. Kass, calls the Book of Genesis "The Beginning of Wisdom." He follows the unfolding story of Abraham's call as the source of the best qualities known to our human race. As a Christian, I see Genesis also as the beginning of the story of salvation, a story that climaxes in the death and resurrection of our LORD Jesus Christ. I am on the same ground with Professor Kass in sensing the cruciality of God's covenant with Abraham and the importance of its being passed on to his descendants. The first link in that process is Abraham's son, Isaac. But Isaac is not an impressively spiritual man, certainly not in comparison with either Abraham or Jacob. And it is at this point that I am so impressed with Rebekah's role. Pragmatically Rebekah is more significant to the covenant in this generation than is Isaac. It is she who knows that "the elder shall serve the younger." As I indicated earlier, I doubt that Isaac could have coped with this idea. In any event, God entrusted it to Rebekah.

This is remarkable, indeed. Rebekah was not raised with a knowledge of God. Her brother Laban worshiped his own gods (Genesis 31:30), and her niece, Rachel, seemed to worship both the LORD God and her childhood gods (31:34). Yet Rebekah "went to inquire of the LORD" in her time of trouble (25:22)—mind you, not simply to complain (a normal human response) but to *inquire*. And when she got her answer, she lived by it through the rest of her life.

Did she do right in conspiring to deceive Isaac? Not by my judgments. But she was neither the first nor the last believer to have faith in God's purposes and believe in their importance but not enough faith to trust God to bring his own plan to pass without human assistance. Politics both human and divine are full of variations on Rebekah's story, the ungodly philosophy that the end justifies the means.

The late scholar and novelist Maurice Samuel describes Rebekah as the "quick-witted, energetic, self-assured girl [who] arrives straight out of the world of idol-worshippers to serve a husband she has never met, sole heir to a blessing outside her experience."[1] Samuel reasons (rightly, I feel) that when Esau sold his birthright to Jacob, it was "not because Jacob bought it—when a man sells his soul, no purchaser acquires it—but because Jacob was left alone to carry the destiny of the blessing."[2] With the same reasoning, Samuel argues that Rebekah did no injustice to her son Esau in the deception that gave the blessing of the firstborn to Jacob. Esau, Samuel says, would never know the difference. "For the rest of his life he would believe himself to be the carrier of the blessing," but without the character to bring it to pass. "Rebekah had to forestall" such a happening, by "a personal deception" that would "prevent a world deception."[3]

Professor Kass says that credit must be given where credit is due:

The true hero of the story is the courageous, tactful, and above all lovingly prudent Rebekah, who conducts affairs always with circumspection, often behind the scenes. . . . Thanks to Rebekah, the new way survives a most severe test; thanks to Rebekah and the generations of women who, inspired by her example, followed in her footsteps, it survives at least to the present day.[4]

I am uncomfortable with some of the particulars of Rebekah's story, but since life offers us no perfect heroes, I gladly claim her as one of my heroes. And it is very clear that God chose to use her.

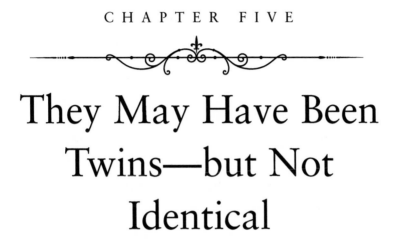

CHAPTER FIVE

They May Have Been Twins—but Not Identical

Scripture Reading: Genesis 29:15-31

Something in our human ego assumes that our generation is the first to know true love. If our parents or grandparents tell us their stories we discount them as quaint and sweet but, of course, not to be compared with our own experiences. It's no wonder, therefore, that we have all sorts of emotional and psychological barriers when we come across love stories in the Bible. And this in spite of the fact that the Old Testament has a full repertoire of romance, some of which becomes quite exotic when it receives television or Hollywood treatment.

I am about to lead us into the story of a romantic triangle involving two sisters, Leah and Rachel, and one man, Jacob, who became husband to both women within a period of eight days. This is story enough, but the plot thickens still more if we accept the theory offered in a fair amount of midrashic literature: Leah and Rachel were twins. ("Midrash" describes the many collections of interpretations and insights on the Hebrew scriptures, from the great sages and scholars of Judaism. It represents the thinking of a number of centuries of such study and teaching.)

Let me begin, however, with the biblical story itself. If you are reading these chapters in order you know that Isaac and Rebekah—grieved that their older son, Esau, had married women in the Canaanite community—told the younger son, Jacob, to go back to the homeland in Haran "and take as wife from there one of the daughters of Laban, your mother's brother." At this point Isaac also spoke the sacred covenant words to Jacob: "May [God] give to you the blessing of Abraham, to you and to your offspring with you, so that you may take possession of the land where you now live as an alien—land that God gave to Abraham" (Genesis 28:4).

In other words this is more than an ordinary trip and
more than an ordinary courtship (if it can be called that).
Jacob is traveling with the divine assignment to carry on the
call that began with his grandfather Abraham more than a
century earlier—a call with implications not only for a
nation that would come from this covenant line but also for
a family that was to bless all humanity.

By foot through wilderness and desert land, Jacob's trip
from his old home to his new one was a journey of some
seventeen days, time enough for Jacob to do a great deal of
thinking. The thinking process got a jump start during
Jacob's first night on the road when in a dream he received
affirmation of the words his father had spoken to him at
his departure. Now, after days of travel, Jacob "saw a well
in the field and three flocks of sheep lying there beside it"
(29:2): a tranquil scene and, in an agrarian world, a perfect
setting for romance.

Jacob had barely learned from the shepherds that he
was indeed in the area where his uncle Laban lived when
Laban's daughter Rachel appeared with her flock of sheep.
Jacob rolled the stone from the well's mouth and apparently
without a word "watered the flock of his mother's brother
Laban" (29:10). The writer of Genesis is careful to give us
this detail specifically, setting the stage for all that is to follow. "Then Jacob kissed Rachel, and wept aloud. And
Jacob told Rachel that he was her father's kinsman, and
that he was Rebekah's son" (29:12). It seems a strange

sequence. We expect that Jacob would introduce himself with the details of the family relationship before kissing Rachel, especially when the kiss includes loud weeping. Rachel must surely have wondered about this stranger, perhaps a bit mad from a journey across the desert, who greets her so intimately and emotionally while providing for her flock. When she receives the information about the family tie, she runs to her father with the news.

Laban welcomes Jacob into his household and after a month he suggests that they enter into a labor contract. At this point Genesis tells us there is more to the family than the shepherd girl Rachel: "Now Laban had two daughters; the name of the elder was Leah, and the name of the younger was Rachel. Leah's eyes were lovely, and Rachel was graceful and beautiful. Jacob loved Rachel" (29:16-18). One has a feeling that Jacob was smitten with Rachel the afternoon he saw her walk to the well with her flocks and that the month of living in her father's household only deepened his feelings. Jacob is quick to suggest a contract. "I will serve you seven years for your younger daughter Rachel" (29:18). Laban answers rather matter-of-factly, "It is better that I give her to you than that I should give her to any other man; stay with me" (29:19). It's the kind of dialogue you might hear in a movie of the old American West, with the father pausing long enough to spit thoughtfully on the ground.

Before we go further into the story we need to look for a moment into the descriptions of Leah and Rachel. The Bible is sparing in its descriptions of people; it tends to tell us a person's actions then lets us draw our conclusions from there. But the writer of Genesis gives us a snapshot of each woman because their physical appearance is significant to the plot and to our fuller understanding of the characters. Rachel, we have read, is "graceful and beautiful," or as the Common English Bible puts it, "a beautiful figure and . . . good looking." The description of Leah speaks only of her eyes, and the descriptive word in the Hebrew is difficult to translate. The New Revised Standard Version says she had "lovely" eyes. The Common English Bible calls her eyes "delicate." Robert Alter, the Hebrew scholar, says "Leah's eyes were tender" and adds in a footnote that the Hebrew word may suggest that "Leah has sweet eyes that are her one asset of appearance, in contrast to her beautiful sister."[1]

So Jacob worked seven years for Rachel but "they seemed to him but a few days because of the love he had for her" (29:20), one of the most romantic sentences in all of literature. Laban arranged a grand wedding and feast, but then he took his daughter Leah to the wedding tent. In the morning Jacob realized that the woman to whom he was married was not Rachel, but Leah. When he complained to his father-in-law, Laban replied, "This is not done in our country—giving the younger before the first-born. Complete the week of this one, and we will give you the other also in return for serving me another seven years" (29:26-27). Obviously Laban had neglected to mention this contractual detail in the earlier conversation, but Jacob had no choice. He married Rachel the following week, and worked for seven years more.

How was Jacob fooled on his wedding night? One element was the darkness, of course, a darkness so complete that we twenty-first-century people can hardly imagine it. It is also more than likely that the feasting included enough wine that Jacob was not in full control of his faculties. The midrashic literature suggests that the girls were twins, and that in the dark there was no distinguishing between the two. Some of the rabbis contended that the two girls conspired together in the matter because Rachel was sympathetic with her older sister and that Rachel whispered to Jacob from outside the tent so that he was hearing her voice in the darkness.

I am impressed, as perhaps you are, that just as Jacob deceived his father in the old man's blindness so that he received the blessing intended for Esau, so now Jacob is deceived in the pitch darkness of night so that he accepts as his wife Leah rather than Rachel. The deceiver has been deceived with the help of darkness. In the contemporary popular phrase, "What goes around comes around"—and in this instance, with touches of irony.

It was not a happy arrangement for Leah. The biblical writer puts it succinctly: Jacob "loved Rachel more than

Leah." Then he adds, "When the LORD saw that Leah was unloved, he opened her womb; but Rachel was barren" (29:30-31). In apparently quick succession Leah has four sons, Reuben, Simeon, Levi, and Judah. It is significant that the names Leah gives the sons not only trace her matrimonial and emotional journey but that in three of the four cases the name also speaks specifically of God. We have every right to conclude that Leah was a woman of admirable faith, a faith that sustained her in a marriage where she was cherished primarily and perhaps only because of her ability to bear children. She named her first child Reuben to express her hope: "Because the LORD has looked on my affliction; surely now my husband will love me" (29:32). She lived with that plaintive hope for the rest of her life, and there is no substantial evidence that her longing was ever truly fulfilled.

The King James Version says that the Lord saw that Leah was "hated" (29:31), but the New Revised Standard Version and other translations say she was "unloved." Most commentators feel that "unloved" is the better term, for it is clear that Jacob wasn't repelled by Leah. But Leah's own feelings were tender, as tender, perhaps, as the eyes that distinguished her. When her second son was born, she named him Simeon because "the LORD has heard that I am hated, he has given me this son also" (29:33). When a human being feels that their only role in the life of another is in their usefulness, whatever its form, it is difficult to distinguish between "unloved" and "hated." Because when our value is only utilitarian we are diminished to a place where we are something less than fully human. That must feel very much like hatred.

Rachel, the graceful and beautiful one, is not accustomed to second place. "When Rachel saw that she bore Jacob no children, she envied her sister." She then cried to Jacob, "Give me children, or I shall die" (30:1). Jacob proves in time that he is a consummate businessman, but this family crisis leaves him undone. Rachel suggests the solution of the ancient world—go to Rachel's maid Bilhah "that she may bear upon my knees" (30:3). Bilhah bears a son whom Rachel names Dan, noting that God has judged her, heard her, and given her a son. Then Bilhah bears a second son. Rachel names this boy Naphtali, meaning for her, "With mighty wrestlings I have wrestled with my sister, and have prevailed" (30:8).

Genesis is making clear that Rachel is motivated not so much by a desire for motherhood or by her love for Jacob as by envy of her sister Leah. Somehow I feel sorry for Rachel. Nature has been generous to her; she is endowed with beauty and charm and probably with those gifts a bewitching self-assurance. When she is surpassed by her older sister at the issue of childbearing, her dominant response is envy. Rachel makes me think of a beautiful American movie star whose adult life suffered a number of disappointments. She regretted, she said, that she was so beautiful so early. Giftedness is a great burden, one which has to be borne with character and grace. Sometimes it is a quality of grace that one can gain only over many years.

Eventually Rachel has a child by her own conception, whom she names Joseph, meaning "He [God] adds"; saying, "May the LORD add to me another son" (30:24). In time Rachel's prayer was answered, and she had a second son. But it was a very difficult birth, to the point of Rachel's dying. "As her soul was departing . . . she named him Ben-oni; but his father called him Benjamin" (35:18). Rachel's name would have meant "Son of my sorrow," but Jacob's revision meant, "Son of the right hand."

Rachel died "on the way to Ephrath," which is now Bethlehem. Jacob set up a pillar to mark her burial place. The writer of Genesis notes that it "is there to this day" (35:20)—that is, to the time when the writer is telling the story. As it happens, the spot is still honored these millennia later. Most contemporary tours of the Holy Land include a stop at Rachel's tomb.

One shouldn't set too much store by what is not said; yet omissions, like the rest stops in music, often make a point. While Genesis tells us clearly at the outset that Jacob loved Rachel, and that the seven years he worked to gain her hand in marriage were like days because of his love for her, it says nothing about the quality of his grief at the time of her death. Indeed, he abrogates her dying wish in the naming of her son, changing the name to fit his own perception.

Rachel's firstborn, Joseph, becomes his father's favorite. Strangely, however, Genesis credits this favoritism not to Joseph's being the son of the beloved Rachel, but "because he was the son of his old age" (37:3). This identification is stranger still since Benjamin was born after Joseph. The writer of Genesis pays Rachel a quiet tribute. When he describes Joseph as "handsome and good-looking" (39:6), he uses the same Hebrew words in the same order as he used earlier to describe Rachel (29:17), though our English translation uses words more fitting to female and male. Clearly, Joseph inherited some of his mother's native attractiveness.

So what shall we say of the sisters Leah and Rachel? Were they twins, as some of the rabbinical literature speculates? We can never know for sure, though there's a fair case in the story of Leah's wedding night, and of course an attractive plot convergence since Jacob was a twin. But they were surely not identical. Rachel was clearly the more beautiful physically and probably the more self-assured and outgoing. If you or I had met them in an ancient marketplace, we would have given first attention to Rachel.

Some writers feel that it was Leah who really loved Jacob. Possibly so. It is certainly clear that she longed for Jacob's love, but of course Rachel didn't need to long for it, because it came to her so easily, as perhaps attention and love often came to Rachel. Leah longed to please Jacob, and bore him six sons and a daughter. One of those sons,

Levi, became the founder of the priestly tribe, and another, Judah, became the one from whom David and the other kings came—and for Christians, the ancestor of Jesus the Christ. When at last Jacob was about to die, he asked his sons to bury him with his ancestors. It would be a long trip from Egypt, but he wanted them to carry him to "the field that Abraham bought from Ephron the Hittite," where Abraham, Sarah, Isaac, and Rebekah were buried and where, Jacob continues, "I buried Leah" (49:30-31).

Finally, what shall we say about the spiritual quality of these two remarkable women, daughters of a clever agricultural entrepreneur and wives of an even more clever husband. Obviously, final judgments of character and of spiritual integrity belong to God alone. But the biblical story gives some hints. Rachel seems to have been opportunistic in her religion. When Jacob announces that he wants to leave his junior partnership with their father, he explains at length how God has blessed him, and Leah and Rachel agree with his plans: "All the property that God has taken away from our father belongs to us and to our children; now then, do whatever God has said to you" (31:16). But as they prepare to leave, "Rachel stole her father's household gods" (31:19) and later she lied to her father in order to keep the gods she had stolen (31:34-35). Rachel's religion was apparently more broad than deep.

It seems to me that Leah was something like her aunt Rebekah, in that though growing up in a pagan world she came to a deep and personal faith in the God of Abraham. Leon Kass, the remarkable scientist who has become a passionate student of Genesis, concludes that Leah "accepted Jacob's God (she speaks of 'the Lord, YHWH')" and that "she speaks of God much more than does Jacob himself."[2]

It was a peculiar family, Jacob, Leah, and Rachel, and one marvels that it managed as well as it did. And Leah and Rachel are interesting prototypes for all the other sisters of history and fiction who have come since. Twins? Perhaps. But each uniquely significant in her own right. And each with her place in the eternal biblical drama.

CHAPTER SIX

The Original
Big Sister

Scripture Reading: Exodus 2:1-10; Numbers 12:1-16

Big sisters are remarkable persons who are easily
maligned. I've had four of them, so I speak with the
authority of experience. Big sisters are quickly drafted to
become assistant mothers; not long after this drafting they
are accused of being bossy. We praise big brothers for
defending younger siblings, but we accuse big sisters of
intruding in other people's business. Big sisters usually get
their most favorable evaluations in retrospect, after the

passage of many years, but even then the praise comes somewhat grudgingly or with a wry smile.

The original big sister was a Hebrew slave girl named Miriam. It is not by chance that her name still has its periods of popularity in the somewhat faddish business of name-giving. She was as crucial an assistant mother as history has ever known and in the process played an irreplaceable role in the making of history. Unfortunately, she reasserted herself as assistant mother when her younger brother was more than eighty years old, much to her eventual pain and embarrassment.

Let's begin the story at the beginning. The family of Jacob (by then known as Israel) migrated to Egypt in a time of widespread famine. The erstwhile star of their family, Joseph, had gotten to Egypt some years earlier by an infamous route in that his brothers had sold him to traveling merchants who in turn sold him into slavery. But Joseph was as brilliant as his dreams and in hardly more than a dozen years he became second in command in all of Egypt, guiding the nation under Pharaoh through prosperity and famine. It was during this famine that his extended family, by that time numbering some seventy people, came to Egypt.

With the passage of generations, however, the people of Egypt forgot Joseph and came to see the family of Israel as dangerous aliens. Their solution was at first to make the Israelites their slaves, implementing massive building programs including the cities of Pithom and Ramses. However, in spite of this repressive measure the Israelite population continued to grow, which of course raised the apprehension of the Egyptian people. Finally the king ordered that every boy born to the Hebrews would be thrown into the Nile River and that only girl babies would be allowed to live.

This edict brought terror to every Israelite family. Nevertheless, when a man and woman from the tribe of Levi had a son, the mother "saw that he was a fine baby" (Exodus 2:2), and wisely or not, she hid him for three months. By that time it was clear they could hide him no longer. The mother got a papyrus basket just the right size for her son, plastered it with bitumen and pitch, then put the infant in this miniature ark and "placed it among the reeds on the bank of the river" (2:2-3). It was a daring venture. The infant was in the keeping of the very river that Pharaoh had appointed as the place of execution for Israel's male babies. By all appearances, now it would be easy for anyone to capsize the little basket and fulfill the king's command.

This is where the big sister, Miriam, comes into the story. She stood nearby, close enough to see what was happening to the baby, to hear his cries, to comfort him, and to scare away a wild animal that might take the child's life, but far enough removed to flee for her life if someone decided to apprehend her. It was a perilous assignment for a

girl just into her teens. One wonders exactly what the
mother had in mind in placing Miriam there. I suspect that
at the least the mother felt that through her daughter she
would learn the baby's fate rather than being left in wondering for the rest of her life. And at the most, perhaps
there would be a miracle.

It was a miracle, and it came through the most unlikely
agency imaginable, or at least the second most unlikely. The
daughter of Pharaoh came to bathe at the river. While she
bathed her attendants walked along the banks. Pharaoh's
daughter saw the tiny boat and asked her maid to fetch it.
When they opened the basket, Pharaoh's daughter saw the
child, saw that he was crying and immediately took pity on
him. "'This must be one of the Hebrews' children,' she
said" (2:6). That is, Pharaoh's daughter recognized that this
was one of the children whose death her father had com-
missioned and this was why the infant was at the river.

Miriam was watching closely, not only listening to every
word but also catching the nuances with which the woman
was speaking. She knew that the woman holding the baby
belonged to the royal family; the entourage made this clear.
I sense that Miriam caught the quality of pity in the manner
of Pharaoh's daughter; she recognized that an Egyptian
woman was at heart as much of a mother as was any
Israelite woman. Culture patterns can influence some of the
structures of motherhood, but there is no ethnicity that
makes a woman less of a mother.

Miriam rose to the occasion. In doing so she was placing her life in the hands of Pharaoh's daughter; after all, alien slaves were a cheap commodity for a woman living in the king's palace. "Shall I go and get you a nurse from the Hebrew women to nurse the child for you," she asked (2:7). Pharaoh's daughter answered simply, "Yes" (2:8).

Had Miriam's mother coached Miriam for the possibility that such a situation might arise? Perhaps. But it is just as likely that Miriam improvised. With no diplomatic script she did business with the king's daughter. And with delicate insight she approached her, not at the level of her royal position but at the quality of her maternal instinct.

Miriam was also sensitive to the culture patterns of her world. An Egyptian woman would not want to nurse an Israelite child, the child of slaves. And just as surely the Israelites wouldn't want their children to be nourished at the breast of an Egyptian. There was a conviction—one that runs very deep in human nature but that was far more intense in the ancient world—that something more than food is transmitted in the process of nursing. Miriam was protecting the ethnic sensitivities of the Egyptians while at the same time satisfying the religious and cultural convictions of her own people.

So it was that a miracle unfolded. Some would call the whole matter a coincidence, others would classify it as a clever scheme on the part of Miriam and her mother. The writer of Exodus offers no opinion. But Exodus is a book that relates God's dealings with the people of Israel in the developing of their responsibility to the rest of the human race. The biblical historian believed that God was at work not only in sparing the life of a Hebrew boy baby but also in the baby's being nursed and tended by his own mother for what was probably the first three years of his life.

The key actor in this miracle vignette was Miriam, the original big sister, but at this point Miriam exits from the story for roughly eighty years. You may have noticed that, as a matter of fact, the writer hasn't mentioned her name. We know her only as the baby's sister. Meanwhile the baby, now known as Moses, the son of Pharaoh's daughter, grows up in the splendor of an Egyptian palace. At this time Egypt was the most powerful nation in the world as we know it and surely the most educationally and culturally advanced. Centuries later, when Stephen, the first Christian martyr, described Moses as "instructed in all the wisdom of the Egyptians and . . . powerful in his words and deeds" (Acts 7:22), we get a clear picture of the world of privilege in which Moses was living.

It was light years removed from the world of Miriam and her contemporaries. The Israelites had become increasingly odious to the Egyptians, so the bondage of their slavery became ever more intense. We imagine that gossip about Moses's life and activities got back to Miriam and her brother Aaron, but we have no evidence to support our imagining. It is clear, however, that somehow Moses kept a sense of his relationship to the Hebrew slaves. Thus one day when "he went out to his people and saw their forced labor" (Exodus 2:11), he saw an act of brutality that enraged him. In his anger he killed an Egyptian overseer. The next day, the son of Pharaoh's daughter became a fugitive. He fled eventually to Midian. There he became a shepherd in the employ of Jethro, married his daughter, and for forty years, followed his flocks on the backside of the desert. Meanwhile Miriam grew old in the world of slavery. A world, however, that had one redeeming quality. Her people somehow kept alive their sense of a covenant with God, and with that covenant a belief that God would eventually fulfill the promises made centuries earlier to Abraham, Isaac, and Jacob. An imaginative writer might also suggest that Miriam kept practicing with her tambourine so that when a day came for celebration, she would be ready to play.

This is Miriam's story, not Moses's, so I'll say just enough about Moses to continue on with Miriam. One day God apprehended Moses when he was tending sheep, doing what he had been doing for some forty years. We should never assume that God is done with us, regardless of our age, and we should never think any location or task is too ordinary for a divine visit. Moses, reluctantly, said yes to God's call and embarked on a series of fierce rejections, sometimes by the people he was trying to help and consistently by the Pharaoh who then ruled.

But eventually Moses led the nation of Israel out of Egypt and through the Red Sea. Moses and the people then sang a grand song of praise and thanksgiving to God. The book of Exodus continues:

> Then the prophet Miriam, Aaron's sister, took a tambourine in her hand, and all the women went out after her with tambourines and with dancing. And Miriam sang to them, "Sing to the Lord, for he has triumphed gloriously; / horse and rider he has thrown into the sea." (Exodus 15:20-21)

You have probably noticed two things in that brief reintroduction of Miriam. First, Exodus calls her "the prophet." This puts her in very select company, especially so early in the biblical story, before prophets became an established part of the work of the Holy Spirit. Second, the writer calls her "Aaron's sister." Why not "Moses's sister"? I have to tell you that I really don't know why. I could speculate, but it would be without much foundation.

I rejoice, however, in this: that the big sister is not forgotten. The girl who stood in the reeds by the Nile River now stands on the far bank of the Red Sea. But of course "stands" is not a sufficient word. Exodus 15:20 tells us that she led the women "with tambourines and with *dancing*" (italics mine). I like that! Miriam has accumulated some years, no doubt years of grievous labor. But she hasn't lost her love of music or the vigor of her dance. And if a critic suggests that nepotism is at work in Miriam's moment of leadership, I insist that she earned this moment of glory when she was a girl in the reeds, and she waited a long, long while to celebrate.

I like Miriam so I wish I could end her story here, dancing on the shores of the Red Sea. It would be a lovely exit for the girl whose astute heroism laid the way for Moses's eventual act as the great emancipator. But talent and status have their built-in peril. I have a standard answer when anyone asks me what kind of bishop, college president, or committee chair a person will be: it depends on how they respond to power. Power is intoxicating, even a little power. It is quite astonishing how quickly the gavel of office can change a mild soul into a tyrant.

We know nothing about the life of Miriam from teenage girl to the dancer and music director at the Red Sea. We don't know if she ever married; there is no reference to a husband, and with the execution of so many boy babies there was a shortage of men. She lived in a world of subjection, but obviously it didn't kill her spirit. When Exodus refers to her as "the prophet Miriam" I speculate that perhaps her contemporaries saw her spiritual stature even before the Red Sea incident.

In any event, a day came when Miriam and Aaron became jealous of their brother, Moses. The issue, they said, was Moses's wife. They found trouble in her because she was a Cushite woman—or to put the issue more clearly, she was not an Israelite. But we sense immediately that this was a strange issue to raise now; Zipporah had been Moses's wife all along. Her father had visited the Israelites and had counseled with Moses, and Moses had profited much from his counsel. Now it is as if Aaron and Miriam said to each other, "Have you noticed that Zipporah is a Cushite?" It is clear that the issue is not Moses's wife but Moses's authority. The siblings said, "Has the LORD spoken only through Moses? Has he not spoken through us also?" (Numbers 12:2).

It isn't hard to imagine details of the conversation. Aaron reminds Miriam that Moses was afraid to lead Israel until God offered to let Aaron speak for him, to which Miriam could reply, in the inflated language most of us use at times: "Why, I practically raised the boy!"

God wasn't pleased with Aaron and Miriam. God explained the difference between prophets in general (including the two siblings) and Moses in particular: God speaks to prophets in visions and dreams; "Not so with my servant Moses"; Moses "beholds the form of the Lord" (12:7-8). When the cloud of the LORD lifted, "Miriam had become leprous, as white as snow" (12:10). Now Aaron pleaded with Moses on behalf of his sister, and Moses pleaded with God. Miriam lived "out of the camp for seven days" (12:14) (the minimum trial time for evaluating possible cases of leprosy), and the camp of Israel did not move until Miriam returned to the camp.

People often ask why judgment fell only on Miriam; after all, Aaron was also part of the rebellion. Some scholars suggest that it is because if Aaron as high priest was outside the camp, the people would be left without his representation before God during that time. Personally, I feel that the judgment fell primarily on Miriam because she led the rebellion. I judge this because in telling the story, the biblical writer mentions Miriam first; it is "Miriam and Aaron" who spoke against Moses. Ancient literature would not mention a woman's name first without reason. Further, it's clear that Aaron was easily influenced. Earlier, when the people came to him at Mount Sinai in Moses's absence, Aaron quickly acquiesced to their requests and made golden calves for worship. I can't imagine Aaron leading a revolt. To Miriam's credit, and also to her danger, she was a strong personality. She didn't lead the women in singing at the Red Sea just because she had a good sense of time and beat.

Moses used Miriam as an object lesson during the closing lectures before his death. When he warned the people to guard against leprous diseases, he underlined his point: "Remember what the LORD your God did to Miriam on your journey out of Egypt" (Deuteronomy 24:9). I don't know that this was the only way Moses could have made his case, but it was a dramatic emphasis.

I'm glad, nevertheless, that this was not the last biblical reference to Miriam. Centuries later as the prophet Micah pleaded with Israel to return to the Lord God, he reminded them of their history as God's people.

"For I brought you up from the land of Egypt,
  And redeemed you from the house of slavery;
And I sent before you Moses, Aaron, and Miriam."
(Micah 6:4)

"And *Miriam*." The big sister gets the recognition she
so deserved. The prophet, inspired by God's Spirit, can't tell
the story of Israel's deliverance without mentioning her
name. She is right there with the little brother whose
papyrus basket she guarded in the reeds of the Nile River.

CHAPTER SEVEN

Israel's First Female Prime Minister

Scripture Reading: Judges 4:1-16

If you're looking for a truly remarkable woman in the Old Testament you can stop your search when you get to Deborah, the woman who used to hold court under a palm tree between Ramah and Bethel, out in the hill country of Ephraim. In time the people called the tree "the palm of Deborah." She was that kind of person. Place her anywhere, and before long, her mark is so indelibly on that place that the inhabitants forget what they once called it and simply give it her name.

Like many remarkable people, Deborah was an original. The Bible doesn't attempt to list her virtues or to tell the secret of her success. It's as if the biblical writer assumes you will understand, either because you've always known about Deborah or because her abilities are self-evident.

They must have been self-evident for her to have become a judge in Israel. As we have noted before, the ancient world was a man's world and nowhere more so than in the halls of power. In those days, power in Israel resided in the judges. After the death of Joshua, the brilliant general who succeeded Moses, there was a vacuum of leadership in the nation. It was a critical time in Israel's history. For several generations they had been a nomadic people, first moving to their promised land and then taking it conquest. Now they must settle the land and become a nation. Surrounding nations, however, didn't cooperate in this enterprise, nor would we expect them to do so. It was to their advantage to destroy Israel before it had opportunity to establish itself.

During those perilous days there was no central government and no structure for selecting leaders or for passing leadership from one generation to another. In Israel the role of leadership was especially complicated because the leader must be not only a person of political and military talent but also someone who could nurture the nation's spiritual responsibilities. Israel was a called nation, a people whose primary purpose was not political or military but spiritual.

They were to carry into the world a unique quality of godliness and of divine purpose.

So who was qualified to lead such a people on such a quest? Some of the persons, like Gideon and Samuel, were dramatically called by God. Others, like Ibzan, Elon, and Abdon, seem like hardly more than fillers for an empty space in the story. Still others were leaders of true genius, yet we know next to nothing about how God called them or why particularly God chose them. Of these several larger-than-life personalities no one is more unlikely and no one given less explanation than the woman Deborah.

The Book of Judges is made up almost entirely of bad times, but few if any were worse than the days when Jabin was king of Canaan, and Sisera was his spectacular general. Sisera had a legendary military force, with nine hundred chariots of iron, and he "oppressed the Israelites cruelly for twenty years" (Judges 4:3). At this point the people of Israel "cried out to the Lord for help" (4:3). This is where we meet Deborah. Her press release is short. She is "a prophetess, wife of Lappidoth," and she was judging Israel under that palm tree (4:4).

The Bible doesn't tell us that God spoke to her; perhaps this is assumed in her being a prophetess. The writer of Judges says simply, "She sent and summoned Barak son of Abinoam from Kedesh in Naphtali, and said to him, 'The LORD, the God of Israel, commands you'" (4:6). I interrupt the sentence midway because the rest is detail. I pause

where I have because the sentence makes clear that
Deborah knew who she was and that she was utterly confident that God was with her. She was so confident of this
that she didn't hesitate to give unqualified orders to the best
military leader in reach, and she was so clearly in command
that General Barak felt no offense at her brisk order.

To the contrary, the general asked only one qualification
in his answer: "If you will go with me, I will go; but if you
will not go with me, I will not go" (4:8). Barak was saying,
"If you are so convinced that I am the person to do this,
then prove it by coming with me." Whatever the meaning
of his statement, it was a quite unlikely word for a military
leader to speak to a woman. Women weren't part of the
military. They kept the home fires burning so that when the
warriors returned there would be a place of celebration in
victory or of solace in defeat. Barak was wise enough to
know that Deborah possessed some intangible qualities that
were essential to their nation's unlikely venture. Israel had
no chance against the superior forces of Canaan; if they
were to have a chance, it lay in this woman Deborah.

The biblical writer gives scanty military details, yet
enough for us to know that Deborah is doing her unique
thing. Barak summons men from the tribes of Zebulon and
Naphtali: "and ten thousand warriors went up behind him;
and Deborah went up with him" (4:10). Just that:
"Deborah went up with him." Barak had insisted that she
go with him, and she did. Meanwhile, General Sisera

"called out all his chariots" (4:13), all nine hundred of them. I assume that this was a dramatic gesture, a bit of military bravado. Sisera hardly needed to bring out the entire elite company of what must have been the most progressive military machinery of his time. Perhaps he calculated that the underequipped volunteers from Israel would simply concede the battle when they saw the sophisticated artillery of their opposition.

But Sisera hadn't reckoned with Deborah. She spoke to Barak. "Up! For this is the day on which the LORD has given Sisera into your hand. The LORD is indeed going out before you" (4:14). This was neither a reasoned discourse nor a military plan. If anything it was a benediction to an ordination service for a general.

Barak responded accordingly. As the writer tells us, he "went down from Mount Tabor with ten thousand warriors following him." What then happened seems to have had little to do with the troops. "And the LORD threw Sisera and all his chariots and all his army into a panic before Barak" (4:15). The panic, in fact, was so great that Sisera got out of his chariot and fled on foot. Of course this added to the humiliating disarray of his forces and their complete demolishing. As for Sisera, he stumbled wearily into the tent of a Kenite woman, a tribal people he thought of as allies, who within hours became his executioner.

Then Barak and Deborah sang a duet. "I will make melody to the LORD, the God of Israel," they sang.

> The peasantry prospered in Israel,
>   they grew fat on plunder,
> because you arose, Deborah,
>   arose as a mother in Israel
> My heart goes out to the commanders of Israel
>   who offered themselves willingly among the people. (5:7, 9)

All of this prosperity came to a culture where previously
"caravans ceased / and travelers kept to the byways" (5:6).
It had been a world where people were afraid to travel and
where normal business had gone into hiding. Because of
Deborah and Barak, however, blessed tranquility came to
the land.

Deborah and Barak's song has a wonderful exuberance,
especially in the iconic line,

> The stars fought from heaven;
>   from their courses they fought against Sisera.
> The torrent Kishon swept them away,
>   the onrushing torrent, the torrent Kishon.
> March on, my soul, with might! (5:20-21)

But their song is also candid. They praise the tribes of
Zebulon and Naphtali because they arose with vigor but
speak with open scorn of Reuben, Gilead, Dan, and Asher,
who waited cautiously to see how it would all turn out.
They pay special tribute to Jael, the Kenite, "of tent-
dwelling women most blessed" (5:24). And they imagine
what passed through the mind of the mother of Sisera
suggesting, probably correctly, the way she was already

counting the spoils for her son. Sisera, as we noted earlier, "had oppressed the Israelites cruelly for twenty years." Now it was Israel's turn to sing in triumph.

So what was Deborah's secret? What made her a forerunner for Joan of Arc and Golda Meir? How is it that this woman came to center stage in a time when the fledgling nation of Israel was most needy and when power was measured almost exclusively in biceps and the limbs of those who could run like deer? The Bible tells us nothing of her physical prowess; she was no female Samson. Nor does it even hint that she was a woman of enchanting beauty, like Rachel before her or Delilah later. Where did God find Deborah, and with what talents did God endow her?

As for where God found her, I suspect it was where God is always finding extraordinary people. God found her in some ordinary place. That's where we find most special people—in quite un-special places. True, the apostle Paul could say that he came from Tarsus, "an important city" (Acts 21:39), but Moses was born in a slave hut in Egypt, and our Lord was born in Bethlehem, a one-street village.

So what were Deborah's special talents? The poem refers to her specifically as "a mother in Israel." We recognize that this is a word of praise but we don't know in what sense the poetry is using the term. Is it referring to her personal family role and with it glorifying motherhood in general? Or is it a kind of political term, to describe the way Deborah watched over her nation as judge and deliverer? And is it suggesting that Israel and all other peoples need a maternal influence, both as individuals and as a culture? One thing is sure, the phrase "a mother in Israel" underlines her unique stake in her nation's future, and it has lived on through the centuries.

Whatever her secret, Deborah had some special magnetism that caused people to turn to her and to trust her. I think it is within my lifetime that the word *charismatic* has become a favorite adjective to link with *leader*. The word has its origins in the New Testament Greek, meaning "gifted." I am always amused just a bit when I hear the word because it strikes me as the kind of word we invent or develop when we have a quality, a situation, a scene, or a person for whom we have no adequate adjective. When we say that someone is a charismatic leader we're saying that they possess some gifts of personality that we can't classify or explain. We know it's there, but when we try to describe it we resort to that ineloquent phrase, "Well, you know." And of course we don't. That's why we fumble for a word that fits and sometimes invent one that fills the gap while leaving us with no more specific knowledge than we had before.

The best thing I know about Deborah is that she was ready for God to use her, and it may be that we need to know no more. The first word the Bible uses to describe her is not leader or judge, but *prophetess*. That is, she was a person to whom God spoke and who then passed on the message. Perhaps instead of describing a prophetess as someone to whom God spoke I should say that she was a person who listened to God. As the years of my life go on I realize that God speaks more often than we know. The problem is not so much that God is silent, but that we are so often inattentive. We humans are so distracted that we just don't hear.

We twenty-first-century people know what distracts us: television, the Internet, Twitter, Facebook, and several other matters that will no doubt come into our vocabularies before these words of mine appear in print. There were distractions in Deborah's time, too; they were called false gods. It may be that the biblical term is more operatively correct than the synonyms we use. In any case, Deborah heard when God spoke and that made all the difference.

So it was that the people of the hill country of Ephraim (a philosophically barren place, I'm sure) came to feel that the wife of Lappidoth knew God in ways they did not, and they sought her counsel. In time the prophetess became a judge, not because they held elections in ancient Israel but because then as always people did the most significant of all voting, the everyday response to what they saw as quality and character. Deborah became a judge because people trusted her and began beating a path to the palm tree between Ramah and Bethel. Deborah was a person of holy gifts and her desperate countrymen recognized this fact. It's quite possible that if they had been prosperous and comfortable they wouldn't have sought out Deborah. I suspect that some of God's prophets have gone unnoticed because they spoke in eras when people were so preoccupied with matters other than God that they weren't interested.

After we have made all our analyses, however, we settle on some common words, clichés even. Deborah was a woman of character, and her character gave her uncommon strength. She was fully committed to God and to her people. She was a woman of great faith, and she was fearless. Her culture was not one in which women were expected to lead, but Deborah forgot that she was a woman and because she forgot it, the people did too. In this, she became more of a woman, not less of one. Because whether we are woman or man, we need always to know that we are, first and most important, human beings.

The Bible tells us that the land had rest for forty years after Deborah and Barak's great victory over the armies of Canaan, and that after those forty years "the Israelites did what was evil in the sight of the LORD" (Judges 6:1). For forty years her influence remained, though no doubt slowly and imperceptibly diminishing. For forty years the herdsmen and families of Israel remembered that they were a different people, called of God through their ancestor Abraham, a people who had survived centuries of forced labor in Egypt, and a people who at times realized, however dimly, that they were to be a light to all the peoples around them.

But it is very difficult to maintain the bright light of idealism in a cloudy world. Just over two hundred years ago the English poet William Wordsworth warned, "The world is too much with us; late and soon, / Getting and spending, we lay waste our powers."[1] Even without automobiles and jet aircraft and computers, Wordsworth's world was a materialistic one, and so was ancient Israel, even in an agricultural economy. It has been hard ever since Eden for us to keep sensitive to the purposes of God. The press of life's insistent ordinariness gets to us.

So after forty years was Deborah a waste, someone of whom we could say, "all is vanity," nothing but a passing breath? By no means. Each generation is priceless in its own right, and God's judgment on us has to do primarily with what we do with the battle of good and evil in our own time. There will be no ultimate victory until the kingdom of God has fully come. Meanwhile you and I are the caretakers of this territory known as The Present. We find ourselves fighting some of the same battles as our faith ancestors have fought since the time of Abraham; the names and garments have changed but the issues remain surprisingly the same.

Deborah won the battle in her day. A remarkable woman, we say, far ahead of her time. She was that. But so it is with all those who love, live, fight, and pray for goodness and justice: they are always ahead of their time. And if they win the battle for forty years, thanks be to God!

Sometimes it is a grand feat to win for forty minutes, especially in the private battlefield of our own souls.

At a certain point in time, like Deborah, you and I will turn the battle over to another generation. Then they will decide whether, how, and to what extent they will follow the Lord God.

CHAPTER EIGHT

The Perfect In-Laws

Scripture Reading: Ruth 1:1-18

When humor was more innocent, even if sometimes insensitive, in-laws were a chosen butt of endless jokes. This is at least partly because humor is a classic way of dealing with the things we cannot change. The wise person learns that we do better to laugh about some matters than to rail hopelessly against them or to grow bitter in thinking of them. To fall in love is to invite into your life not only the person you love but also all of those persons who are related to the one you love. Sometimes this enlarges life wonderfully. But even at best it also complicates life. In my years as a pastor, officiating at hundreds of weddings, I usually reminded the prospective bride and groom that they were marrying not only each other but also each other's families. (And indeed also their circle of friends, associates, and hangers-on.) But the in-laws are most important, simply because they have a relationship with the bride and groom by both blood and sentiment.

Since in-laws are such a delicate matter and often a source of tension, it is fascinating that one of the most beautiful and eloquent expressions of love in any language was a declaration by a daughter-in-law to her mother-in-law. We quote this statement in many wedding ceremonies, though frequently those who hear it think that it is a word from bride to groom or groom to bride rather than a statement between in-laws.

The story of the perfect in-laws comes to us in the little Book of Ruth. A Bible teacher of my youth from whom I learned much described this book as the silver lining to the book of Judges. If you know anything about the Book of Judges, you know that it needs a silver lining, because most of it is a record of difficult times, when the new nation of Israel was struggling to establish itself in the midst of more settled nations, which were doing everything possible to put an end to Israel.

In the Book of Ruth nature seemed to join the conspiracy against Israel. Hear the opening sentence: "In the days when the judges ruled, there was a famine in the land" (Ruth 1:1). This is what some folks would call a double

whammy: political/military disaster compounded by vengeful nature. The days of the judges were almost always difficult, and now nature was difficult too. So "a certain man in
Bethlehem" (1:1) acted audaciously, out of desperation. He
moved, with his wife Naomi and his two sons, Mahlon and
Chilion, to Moab. It isn't that Moab was that distant a trip,
though any travel was tedious and trying in those days. The
point is that Israelites didn't like to leave their homeland
because their tie to particular plots was both hereditary and
sacred; and still worse, if an Israelite were going to migrate
anywhere, it surely wouldn't be to Moab. There was a
longstanding enmity between the two peoples. When Israel
was escaping from Egypt, the Moabites "did not meet
[them] with food and water"; instead they hired Balaam to
curse them. As a result, Moses commanded Israel that they
should not admit any Moabite into their assembly "even to
the tenth generation" (Deuteronomy 23:3-6).

But hard times sometimes make people forget ancient
prejudices; this "certain man in Bethlehem" and his family
moved to Moab. Elimelech was his name, and the author
mentions it only later. This may be significant. His name
means "to me shall kingship come," which causes some
scholars to feel that perhaps Elimelech thought unduly well
of himself, to a point where he would leave his homeland
rather than deal with hardship.

This is, of course, only speculation. What we do know
is that after the family moved to Moab, they "remained

there," which suggests that though the famine in their homeland was past, Moab had become home to Elimelech, Naomi, and their sons. When Elimelech died, the two boys married Moabite girls, Orpah and Ruth. Clearly, they had decided to make Moab their home; Bethlehem was no longer in their thinking.

But then the two sons died. If we were reading this story in the Hebrew, we wouldn't be surprised because their names, Mahlon ("diseased") and Chilion ("perishing"), suggest that they were sickly from birth. So now we have three widows in a world where women depended on men for their sustenance. There was no career awaiting any of the three, no provision for transition to a new life. A hope did remain, however, for Naomi, the mother-in-law. Back in Bethlehem there was still her husband's tribal land, apparently heavily mortgaged; and there was also a relative of her late husband who bore a responsibility under Israel's law to redeem the land and marry the widow who had claim to the land. Naomi did not just do a wise thing, she did the only thing. She decided to move back to Bethlehem.

It is here that the in-law factor asserts itself. The three women set out together for Naomi's homeland. But Naomi thought better of the matter. "Go back each of you to your mother's house. May the LORD deal kindly with you, as you have dealt with the dead and with me. May the LORD grant that you may find security, each of you in the house of your husband" (1:8-9). Naomi was giving good counsel. The two

Moabite girls were not likely to be welcome in Israel and were even less likely to find marriage there. If there was to be security for Orpah and Ruth it would be in Moab, with a Moabite husband.

The women kissed and wept. They loved one another. They had bonded—first as a family of marriage and now in the ties of mutual loss and pain. The daughters-in-law became insistent. "No, we will return with you to your people" (1:10). Again, Naomi is realistic. She puts the matter baldly:

> Turn back, my daughters, why will you go with me? Do I still have sons in my womb that they may become your husbands? Turn back, my daughters, go your way, for I am too old to have a husband. Even if I thought there was hope for me, even if I should have a husband tonight and bear sons, would you then wait until they were grown? (Ruth 1:11-13)

Naomi was referring to the law of her people, that if she had sons they were to take up marital responsibility to the widows since the original husbands had not had children. Under such circumstances the first child born to the new marriage would rank legally as heir to the widow's first husband.

Then Naomi added a sentence that would have convinced me to turn around if I were her in-law. "No, my daughters, it has been far more bitter for me than for you, because the hand of the LORD has turned against me" (1:13). Naomi is justified in feeling that she has suffered even more than the two younger women, since she has lost two sons as well as her husband. But I am uneasy with the line that follows: "because the hand of the LORD has turned against me." Naomi has developed an attitude of life, with a theological base to support it, that almost guarantees her being unhappy for the rest of her life. The person who chooses to join Naomi is not taking on a delightful travel companion.

Orpah is reasonable. The three women burst into tears again, then Orpah kisses her mother-in-law and departs, but Ruth clings to her. She has heard her mother-in-law's argument and she knows it is logical. She knows well enough that there is no future in Naomi. But Ruth is one of those persons who makes her judgment not on the basis of logic or personal well-being but on love and loyalty. She makes her point of stubborn love in some of the most beautiful language ever written.

> Do not press me to leave you
>   Or to turn back from following you!
> Where you go, I will go;
>   Where you lodge, I will lodge;
> your people shall be my people,
>   and your God my God.
> Where you die, I will die —
>   there will I be buried.
> May the LORD do thus and so to me,
>   and more as well,
> if even death parts me from you! (Ruth 1:16-17)

The narrator tells us, "When Naomi saw that she was determined to go with her, she said no more to her" (1:18).

We don't have any details about the tedious, tiring walk from Moab to Bethlehem, but we learn quickly that even Ruth's loyalty hasn't changed Naomi's outlook. As the two women come to Bethlehem, the town "was stirred because of them." The women of the town ask, "Is this Naomi?" (1:19). Their question is a reasonable one; she has been gone a long time, long enough for her sons to grow up and marry and die and for her husband to die as well. Naomi has grown older, no doubt about that. But her personality has changed too, and with all that has happened to her, we shouldn't judge her too harshly. Nevertheless, her answer is not a cheerful one, and it isn't true to her name, Naomi, which means "pleasant."

> Call me no longer Naomi [pleasant],
>   call me Mara [bitter],
>   for the Almighty has dealt bitterly with me.
> I went away full,
>   but the LORD has brought me back empty;
> why call me Naomi
>   when the LORD has dealt harshly with me,
>   and the Almighty has brought calamity upon me?
> (Ruth 1:20-21)

At this point Naomi may not be a bundle of joy but neither has she lost her instinct for survival. The time is propitious; it is the time of the barley harvest. This meant temporary employment, though it was the employment of mercy. According to the laws of Israel, at harvest time, owners and their workers were to harvest the crops generously, leaving corners of the fields and other places untouched so that the poor could follow after them, gleaning the leftovers. Ruth is hopeful. "Let me go to the field and glean among the ears of grain, behind someone in whose sight I may find favour." Naomi answers to the point: "Go, my daughter" (2:2).

The biblical writer has already hinted that God is at work. He tells us that Naomi had a kinsman on Elimelech's side, "a prominent rich man" (2:1), named Boaz. We read a few sentences later, "As it happened, [Ruth] came to the part of the field belonging to Boaz" (2:3). As I read that sentence I remember a lecture I heard more than half a century ago in which the speaker recited his experiences traveling through Europe soon after World War II. He punctuated the lecture at regular intervals with the question, "Coincidence? Or Providence?" You can take your choice in this story. Obviously, the biblical writer expects you to answer "Providence."

But sometimes even God's providence demands human cooperation. When Boaz inquired about the young woman (who seemed to stand out among the gleaners), the servant in charge of the reapers not only identified who she was but also reported that she had been "on her feet from early this morning until now, without resting even for a moment" (2:7). With that good report, Boaz approached Ruth and counseled her to stay close to his women workers. He also warned the young men not to bother her; an attractive young alien woman could be easy prey. And Ruth did nothing to hide her social handicap, thanking Boaz for taking notice of her, "a foreigner" (2:10).

Now Boaz indicates that he has done his research. He knows that Ruth has left her parents and her native land to come "to a people that you did not know before"; then he puts her experience in a faith dimension: "may you have a full reward from the LORD, the God of Israel, under whose wings you have come for refuge" (2:12)! Part of Ruth's announcement to her mother-in-law was that "your God [shall be] my God" (1:16). Of all the ways that Ruth broke from her past in going with Naomi, this was the most significant; she was accepting Naomi's God. Boaz now blesses Ruth in the name of the LORD God of Israel. This is his acknowledgment that the Moabite girl is now part of the people of Israel, whose law would otherwise make her an outcast to the tenth generation.

Well, I think you know what happens next. It would be fun to stretch out the story, and a romance novelist could make several hundred pages of it I'm sure. When Naomi learns that Boaz has shown this extraordinary interest in Ruth, she becomes a full-scale matchmaker. If there was in the past any reluctance or timidity on Boaz's part, Naomi will see to it that such impediments are removed. Boaz himself takes care of a crucial legal impediment, and the two are married to the great pleasure of all the people of Bethlehem. In time they have a son, Obed, and the last line of the book of Ruth reminds us of something he had already said in the previous paragraph, that Obed's grandson is David. The writer doesn't tell us that this is *the* David, Israel's iconic king, because he doesn't have to; any good Jewish reader will know as much.

So what made Naomi and Ruth such perfect in-laws? Some crucial factors were against it. Especially there was the age-old political enmity between their two peoples, Moab and Israel, to which I have referred earlier. All of us inherit some prejudices, though we may not name them as such. As I travel about the United States I discover that some football fans whose loyalty is to Alabama's Crimson Tide can hardly imagine a son or daughter marrying into Auburn alumni, just as those devoted to the University of Michigan avoid any ties to fans of Ohio State. But it was a life-and-death feeling in Israel and Moab, and old feelings taint continuing generations more than they know. Also, even the best mother-in-law and daughter-in-law can be jealous for the affection of the son/husband.

So what brought the two women together? Human need, for one thing. Your mother told you, "Misery loves company." The Oxford Dictionary of Quotations dates that folk wisdom to the late sixteenth century, but all of us know that Eve must have said it to one of her kin. Mutual pain drew Naomi and Ruth together. But of course Orpah

knew the same pain, so there were other elements at work
for the perfect in-laws.

If I were a psychologist or a social scientist I would venture opinions about the laws of friendship, those things that
draw people together. But in my long life I've had too much
experience with friendship to trust any such laws or studies
or surveys. We can explain some of our friendships—ethnic
ties, common interests, intellectual compatibility—but some
of our best friendships develop outside all logic.

I understand Naomi and Ruth on the ground of their
religious faith. Some of you will conclude that I speak from
prejudice because my faith means so much to me, and you
may be right. But when I hear Ruth recite her pledge to her
mother-in-law, I conclude that the crucial line is this: "your
God my God." This is more important even than "your
people shall be my people," because Ruth couldn't accept
Naomi's people without accepting Naomi's God. It was the
God of Israel that made Israel different from all the nations
around them. The people of Israel knew this and sometimes
found it embarrassing and troublesome, but they couldn't
shake it for long. Their holy days, their rituals, and their
insistent, vigorous prophets wouldn't let them—nor would
their enemies.

I believe Orpah had as good reason to love Naomi as
did Ruth. I think the bond that tied Ruth and Naomi insep-
arably was the bond that came when Ruth accepted
Naomi's God as her God. I don't know when she did this,

but it was no mere formality, no calculated benefit (indeed, a burden in what it did to Ruth's relationship to her birth people), and no temporary enthusiasm. It was a direction-changing, life-shaping choice.

As a result, Ruth traveled a trying road from Moab to Bethlehem, took a life-and-death gamble on the future, opened herself to rejection by a naturally enemy people, and ended up being the wife of an adoring older husband, the mother of a cherished son, the great grandmother of Israel's greatest king (4:17, 22), and an ancestress of Jesus Christ (Matthew 1:5).

That's an in-law story that puts a pause on all in-law jokes.

CHAPTER NINE

The Ladies' Chorus

Scripture Reading: Ruth 4:13-17

If you think I'm a dreamer, an idealist, and a romantic, I plead guilty. More than that, I'd be ashamed to be less. I am also a believer in little people, those who live out their lives in relatively obscure places. Those were the people with whom I grew up, my neighbors to the right and the left on Center Street and West Palmer and lower Fourth Street. This explains why I'm giving over a chapter of this book to an anonymous group that the Bible calls "the women." I realize that I have a limited number of chapters in this book, and I confess that I am leaving out several women I would dearly love to include. But my soul would not be at peace if I did not pay credit to the women of the chorus.

Like the story of the perfect in-laws, the bright and shining moment for the women of the chorus comes to us in the Old Testament book of Ruth. We don't know who the judge was in Israel at that time, but since the writer doesn't mention the name I'm inclined to think that it was probably one of those almost-nonentities, like Shamgar, Tola, or Jair. Nothing spectacular was happening on the political or military scene, and sometimes that's the best of times for folks who are simply trying to raise their crops, tend their shops, and do right by their families.

You don't have to be a dreamer or a romantic to believe that important things may be happening in inauspicious times and places. All you need is a little knowledge of history. I often recall a newspaper cartoon on some February 12 from my childhood, titled "1809." If I remember rightly, the cartoon featured a picture of two men visiting in a crude frontier store: "Any news this morning?" "Not much, though I hear Tom Lincoln's wife had a baby boy." I think too of some spring day in the mid-nineteenth century when an eight- or nine-year-old boy, son of a slave woman, was planting a garden in rural Missouri. Would anyone have guessed that it was the start of the career of one of history's greatest scientists, George Washington Carver? Who knows when great things are happening in quiet times and obscure places?

The story of the women's chorus begins in the events we discussed in the preceding chapter. The women of Bethlehem bid farewell to one of their favorite members, Naomi. Why am I so sure that she was one of their favorites? I get this idea from her name, which meant "pleasant." The name fit. When famine hit the area, Naomi's husband decided to seek the family fortune in Moab. The Bible tells us nothing about how the women of Bethlehem responded to Naomi's move, but it isn't hard to imagine. Foremost, they hated to see her go. They would miss her bright and sometimes biting comments in morning conversations at the town well. Also, they were skeptical about the move to Moab. Why would Naomi's husband move the family into foreign and generally hostile territory? Why not stick it out, the way the rest of them were doing, holding things together in famine until better times? "No good will come of this move," some women no doubt said; and they may have spoken with sympathy for Naomi or with ill-concealed anger for Elimelech, her husband.

As time passed by, occasional reports came back from Moab. The family was staying in Moab; apparently Elimelech liked it there. Then they heard that Elimelech died and, before long, that the two boys had married Moabite girls; and the women of Bethlehem said at the well, "We knew no good would come of this move." What good ever happened in Moab? The women of Moab had been seducing Israelite men since the days of Moses.

99

Then, in what seemed a very short time, there was news that one of Naomi's sons had died ("He was always sickly," the women may have said), and then the other. Now all speculation turned to sorrow and sympathy. What would poor Naomi do, a widow with two widow daughters-in-law, in a strange land? Where would she turn now? The answer came on a day when two women appeared in Bethlehem; "the whole town was stirred because of them," the Bible tells us; and the biblical writer specifically quotes the women: "Is this Naomi?" they asked (Ruth 1:19).

The answer was yes and no. She was older, of course, but there was no doubt, this was Naomi. And yet, she wasn't. She said so herself.

> Call me no longer Naomi [pleasant],
>   call me Mara [bitter],
>   for the Almighty has dealt bitterly with me. (1:20)

This wasn't the woman who had left them some years back, the woman always full of hope, ready even to go with her husband on a questionable relocation years ago. The sharpness of her speech was still there, but it had lost its lovely edge, the smile that made her clever comments cute. Her faith had changed too. At times Naomi may have watched God with a wary eye, but she always came out on the side of trust. Now she was directing her complaints at God, as if he had taken a personal disliking to her.

As for the daughter-in-law, the Moabite girl named Ruth, she wasn't as bad as they expected. True, she was a bit prettier than a widow should be, but of course she was still young. And yes, like those proverbial Moabite women, she had a bit of a flair ("You can see why Naomi's son was attracted to her"). But she had a lovely smile. And she wasn't pushy. Look at her arms; she's used to work. Above all, though, the women noticed the girl's attention to Naomi. It was more than obligation; it was true affection. This Moabite girl actually cared about their old friend, Naomi, even though Naomi wasn't pleasant anymore.

The women didn't need long to get more of the story. Both of the daughters-in-law were good women, Naomi said; she couldn't have asked for better girls. But after the deaths of the three men, she had pleaded with them both to return to their own people.

> I had nothing to offer them, no children in my womb. The other girl, Orpah, had finally agreed, but not Ruth. She wouldn't listen to reason. She loved me [this with a self-deprecating shrug of the shoulders]. But I saw something else. She loved our God. Somehow she had come to love the God of Israel. No matter the world in which she was raised, and their gods: she loved the Lord God and he was now her God too.

The women of Bethlehem noticed that Ruth allowed no delay before going to work among the gleaners, expecting no favors and making clear that her mother-in-law shouldn't do such work. And they heard from the reapers that the girl was tireless; friendly, but with no time for small talk. Then, quickly, there were rumors. Boaz, the owner of the field, had noticed the girl. He had advised his foremen to keep her from predators. Some speculated that Boaz was a lonely man.

Then there were facts to go with the rumors. Boaz was kin to Elimelech, Naomi's late husband, and to her deceased sons, Mahlon and Chilion, so by levitical law he bore a responsibility to her property. But there was a relative who was nearer kin than Boaz; he had first claim. So Boaz watched for him at the city gate, and with ten elders as witnesses explained the situation. "Naomi, who has come back from the country of Moab, is selling the parcel of land that belonged to our kinsman Elimelech"(4:3). Boaz explained that the first rights belonged to this man and that if he didn't buy, Boaz wanted to do so. The man quickly answered, "I will redeem it" (4:4). Then Boaz reminded the man of another fact of the levitical law. "The day you acquire the field from the hand of Naomi, you are also acquiring Ruth the Moabite, the widow of the dead man, to maintain the dead man's name on his inheritance" (4:5).

The anonymous kin quickly pulled back from the proposed purchase. The Bible tells us that in those days it was the custom at this point in a transaction for the one person to take off a sandal and give it to the other person. Boaz accepted the sandal and announced to the assembled group,

> Today you are witnesses that I have acquired from the hand of Naomi all that belonged to Elimelech and all that belonged to Chilion and Mahlon. I have also acquired Ruth the Moabite, the wife of Mahlon, to be my wife, to main-

tain the dead man's name on his inheritance, in order that
the name of the dead may not be cut off from his kindred
and from the gate of his native place; today you are
witnesses. (4:9-10)

The story seems quaint in its details and offensive when
it says that Boaz "acquired Ruth," as if she were a piece of
the property. But we should ponder some positive elements;
such as, the sense of family responsibility. When hard times
came, whether by famine or the economy or war or sick-
ness and death, the nearest kin was expected to respond.
This responsibility included women of the household, for
whom the ancient culture, mostly agricultural, provided no
career opportunities for women. And there was a sense of
respect for the dead. If a married man had died without
children, the next of kin and the community saw the first
child born to the new union as the descendant of the
deceased. The sense of family and of family responsibility
was paramount in ancient Israel.

The people of Bethlehem rejoiced in the little legal cere-
mony that had just taken place. Not just the elders who
had been called in to witness the discussion but also "all
the people who were at the gate" (4:10) joined in a blessing. And it was a blessing not on the land Boaz had
redeemed, but on Ruth, the young widow he was about to
marry.

May the LORD make the woman who is coming into your
house like Rachel and Leah, who together built up the

house of Israel. May you produce children in Ephrathah and bestow a name in Bethlehem; and, through the children that the LORD will give you by this young woman, may your house be like the house of Perez, whom Tamar bore to Judah. (4:11-12)

It was a strange and wonderful blessing. On the human side there is an implicit congratulation to Boaz, an older man, on his marriage to "this young woman." The blessing is grand and far-reaching in its reference to Rachel and Leah, the wives of Jacob, and the legal tie to Israel's twelve tribes. Then there is the rather unlikely reference to "Perez, whom Tamar bore to Judah." You will find the details of that union and birth in a chapter of the Bible that we don't usually include in Sunday school studies, Genesis 38. It is such an important story, however, that the opening chapter of the New Testament mentions Tamar and Perez (Matthew 1:3).

The Bible makes clear that Ruth and Boaz are no ordinary couple. Students of literature often describe the book of Ruth as the most beautiful love story ever written, or one of the most beautiful. And with good reason, because it is such a complete love story, including a tender but candid story not only of the love of woman and man but also of the kind of love that shows itself in deathless loyalty, in Ruth and Naomi. And as short as the book is, there's still plenty of trouble, days of hopelessness, and intrigue.

But the writer wants us to know, above all, that God is at work. So when he reports that "they came together," he continues, "the LORD made her conceive, and she bore a son" (4:13, emphasis added). It is at this point that the ladies' chorus comes into its own. And they center their attention not so much on the baby or the mother but on the grandmother, their old friend and fellow chorus member, Naomi. They spoke their recitation to her:

> Blessed be the LORD who has not left you this day without next-of-kin, and may his name be renowned in Israel! He shall be to you a restorer of life and a nourisher of your old age; for your daughter-in-law who loves you, and is more to you than seven sons, has borne him. (4:14-15)

These women who had grown up with Naomi and had wept for her, if not with her, in the deaths of her husband and sons and who had feared that she would never have descendants were now able to rejoice with her. They saw this as the goodness of God, and practical women that they were, they were glad that Naomi now had provision for her "old age." And they gave a vigorous back of the hand to their old prejudice against the Moabites: they describe Ruth as better than seven sons, and rejoice that it is she who has borne this son to Naomi. They don't give particular notice to Boaz, but of course it is in Naomi that they hold a special stake of love and association. This was all the encouragement Naomi needed. She "took the child and laid him in her bosom, and became his nurse" (4:16).

But the women of the chorus aren't done. They take upon themselves an astonishing privilege: "The women of the neighbourhood gave him a name, saying, 'A son has been born to Naomi.' They named him Obed" (4:17). The writer is being very direct about this. He doesn't say that they suggested this name to Naomi, Ruth, and Boaz, it simply reports that they gave the child its name, as if it were their right and responsibility to do so.

More than that, the women of the chorus said of the child, "A son has been born to Naomi" (4:17). They were speaking, certainly, out of their love and concern for Naomi, but they were also reflecting their sense of community and of family continuity. These qualities are not as significant in our contemporary culture; as a result we find it hard to understand the spirit with which these women of Bethlehem spoke. We tend to be a displaced people, partly by our neglect, partly because of the speed with which we live, and partly because our values have changed. Our individualism has hurt our wider sense of belonging.

When we lose our sense of the past or diminish its importance we lose something of our vision for the future. The biblical writer puts the birth of Obed into its community context, and more than that, into its place in the divine plan. So he writes, "They named him Obed; he became the father of Jesse, the father of David" (4:17). This is the dramatic end to the story, the inspired writer's way of telling us that this is the reason for his telling about Naomi and Elimelech and Ruth and Boaz, because out of all this comes Israel's greatest king. Then the scholar takes over from the dramatist, and the writer recites again the line from Perez to David.

But I love the ladies' chorus. We don't know the name of a single one. They are as obscure as village people from three millennia ago can be. Nevertheless, they are the voice of the community. There's something wonderfully democratic in their naming the child that was born to Ruth and Boaz, and in their rejoicing in the victory, against all odds, of their widowed and bereaved friend, Naomi.

I like choruses! For two years in long ago days I was part of the male quartet that represented our high school in music contests, and once in the mixed octet; and in a year of talent drought, I was the bass soloist. But none of this compares with the experience of singing in the a cappella choir: to turn seventy pairs of eyes with singular attention to an earnest director and feeling the shiver of pleasure that we were all on key. If any voice had stood out, it would have been a violation of who we were. Our business was to contribute fadelessly to the sound of the whole.

The women of Bethlehem did this. But as you see, they belonged not only to the ladies' chorus of their time and place but also to the community of faith that preceded them and to the unfolding purposes of God that would follow them. There's much to be said for a true ladies' chorus. And come to think of it, I like mixed choruses too.

CHAPTER TEN

The Woman Who Saved a King

Scripture Reading: 1 Samuel 25:1-42

When we think of the great personalities of the Old Testament, King David ranks somewhere in the top five, along with Abraham and Moses. The biblical writers used him as the measure of excellence for all the kings of Israel and Judah who followed him. Today, millennia later, the nation of Israel celebrates his memory by the Star of David on its flag. Even a casual reader of the Bible feels a kinship with him, thinking of him as the author of beloved psalms. Every year tens of thousands of parents in every part of the world give a variation of his name to their sons. He is iconic as shepherd, warrior, king, poet, and lover.

But as one might expect with a person of such wide-ranging talents and such a complex personality, he was also tempestuous and unpredictable. He was sunshine and he was cyclone, and no psychological meteorologist could predict which to expect next. With such a personality he could as easily have been a casual accident of history as one of its mythical figures. All of us have someone in our circle of family or friends who but for one poor decision, one inept conversation, one turn in the road might have had their own small story of success. It isn't necessarily an overactive imagination when somebody says, "You know, I could have been (a major league baseball player, president of that company, married to that person) if it hadn't been for . . ." Sometimes it's true.

In the grand purposes of God, David became what he did. But if it hadn't been for God's watchful care (or a kindly Providence, if you prefer), David might never have made it. The name of that divine intervention was Abigail.

It all happened at a sensitive time in David's life. It is not incidental that the biblical writer begins the story, "Now Samuel died," then after noting that the nation mourned Samuel's passing, goes on to say that "David got up and went down to the wilderness of Paran" (1 Samuel 25:1). Samuel's death was a loss to everyone in Israel from

the hard-scrabble farmer to the king, but to no one more
than David. It was Samuel who had come to the farm of
David's father, Jesse, one ominous day, in a search that
brought David in from tending his father's flocks because
Samuel had come on a mission from God. That day Samuel
anointed David as the future king of Israel. The situation
was so irregular and so far distant and far reaching that no
one but David and Samuel could understand what had happened. During the years that followed, David had every reason to wonder if the whole experience was a kind of
adolescent mirage.

David must have been at such a point in his life at the
time of Samuel's death. The idea of his ever becoming King
of Israel seemed less than remote. Instead David was a fugitive from King Saul's wrath, making a living in a way that
is hard to imagine in our world and that was probably marginal even in his. He had gathered around himself several
hundred disaffected young men, the kind that modern soci-
ologists might use for a sophisticated statistical study. In the
language of the biblical writer, "Everyone who was in dis-
tress, and everyone who was in debt, and everyone who
was discontented gathered to him, and he became captain
over them" (22:2). After leading this group for several
years David must have found kingship in Israel a walk in
the park.

This group made their living some of the time as military mercenaries, available where needed and at a price. At

other times, they served as a kind of independent protective agency. They stationed themselves near some major property owner and without contract protected the person's flocks and herds and general holdings from marauders, then in time presented themselves to the landowner for payment. In this instance they chose "a man in Maon, whose property was in Carmel. The man was very rich; he had three thousand sheep and a thousand goats" (25:2). After protecting these holdings for a period of time, David sent ten of his young men to the owner, Nabal, requesting "whatever you have at hand" (25:8). I repeat, it was a strange sort of business. If you read David's complete message you sense that David was saying essentially, "We didn't cause you any trouble and we prevented anyone else from doing so; now how would you like to reward us?"

The Bible tells us that Nabal was a surly, mean man. We also learn that his name meant "fool" and that he was true to his name. Nabal not only refused David's request, he did so with a churlish flourish; one of his servants said that he "shouted insults" (25:14) at David's delegation. Whatever Nabal's style, he had a case. After all, he hadn't hired David's services, and even though business was often done that way, he had a right to refuse it. Furthermore, Nabal no doubt knew a little about the current political scene; a person of his wealth wasn't likely to be in the dark in such matters. He had to know that David was currently in disfavor with King Saul, and Nabal had reason to lean toward Saul rather than a young warrior who was running a marginal business.

David took high umbrage at Nabal's answer. He said to his men, "Every man strap on his sword" (25:13), and they did so: four hundred young men who delighted in mayhem and who hadn't had opportunity recently to exercise that delight. This is David the cyclone; Nabal's property is about to become a disaster area.

Enter Abigail. The Bible says that she was "clever and beautiful" (25:3). Such a combination is hard to beat. One wonders how she happened to be married to a man like Nabal, but such things happen, and not only in the world of arranged marriages. One of Nabal's servants brought the news to Abigail. He told how well David's men had conducted themselves: "they were a wall to us both by night and by day," but now Nabal was inviting disaster and "he is so ill-natured that no one can speak to him" (25:17).

Abigail was not only clever but also able to act with executive decisiveness. She immediately brought together "two hundred loaves of bread, two skins of wine, five sheep ready dressed, five measures of parched grain, one hundred clusters of raisins, and two hundred cakes of figs" (25:18), loaded them on donkeys and sent them ahead to David, and she followed. When she saw David, Abigail "alighted from the donkey, and fell before David on her face, bowing to the ground" (25:23). She then assumed all the blame for what had happened, though acknowledging that Nabal was an "ill-natured fellow: . . . Nabal is his name and folly is with him" (25:25). She prayed for David's welfare: "If anyone should rise up to pursue you and to seek your life, the life of my lord shall be bound in the bundle of the living under the care of the LORD your God" (25:29).

Let me interrupt the story to observe that Abigail's language may seem extravagant to the twenty-first-century world and her physical action decidedly overdone. Make an allowance for differences in time and custom and style, but remember this: graciousness is never out of style. More than that, graciousness is often hard to come by these days, and our world could use more of it. In the words of Mary Poppins, a little bit of sugar helps the medicine go down. I often have the feeling that some of our political discourse could use less bellowing and strutting and more bowing and smiling.

Abigail won the day—resoundingly, in fact. When she returned to Nabal he was having a feast "like the feast of a king," and he was "very drunk; so she told him nothing at all until the morning light" (25:39). When Nabal got the whole story, he also got a stroke of rare good sense, "and his heart died within him; he became like a stone" (25:36-37). Ten days later, he died.

When the news reached David, he got an inspiration of his own. He "sent and wooed Abigail" (25:39) and shortly proposed. They were soon married. As the biblical record shows, David did more marrying than he should have, and he didn't always do it well. In my opinion, Abigail outdistanced all the rest. She didn't have the royal blood of Michal, King Saul's daughter, and probably not the devastating beauty of Bathsheba, but as already said, she was "clever and beautiful," with the kind of intelligence that shapes the contours of the face in hard-to-define ways. I wish Hollywood had chosen this story over David and Bathsheba.

But I haven't told Abigail's story for romantic reasons, much as it must seem just now to be so. My interest is in Abigail's insight regarding David's future, and especially a particular sentence. She notes that the Lord will make of David "a sure house" because David is "fighting the battles of the LORD" (25:28). She realizes, whether by instinct, by divine revelation, or because someone has communicated information to her, that God has spoken good concerning David and "has appointed you prince over Israel" (25:30). And because all of this is true, she wants to be sure that David "shall have no cause of grief, or pangs of conscience, for having shed blood without cause or for having saved himself" (25:31).

We think of David as a robust warrior, conqueror of Goliath, and, in this case, a leader of fractious men. But he was also sensitive enough to be a poet and diplomat enough to maintain a wide variety of friendships. When he heard of Nabal's death, David thanked God that he "has kept back his servant from evil" (25:39). The Lord did, indeed, keep

David back from evil, and it is significant that the next sentence after David's prayer is the report that he set out to woo Abigail, because the instrument by which God held David back from evil was the counsel of that "clever and beautiful" woman.

This is why I dare to say that Abigail is a woman who saved a king. Some people's theology is such that they will insist that David was in the plan of God and that he would therefore become king no matter what. Perhaps so. But it seems clear to me that at this point in his career David was in danger of seriously complicating the purposes of God and that God used a particular human instrument, the woman named Abigail, to keep David on track.

New York City's memorable Mayor Fiorello LaGuardia famously said, "When I make a mistake, it's a beaut!"[1] The size of our mistakes is magnified by the offices we hold simply because the results are more far-reaching. Thus the lapse by a national political leader is especially significant—and so, too, at other levels: those of a teacher, a pastor, an executive, or a parent. But there's more to the story. It is also true that persons in positions of particular responsibility are more susceptible to egregious mistakes; the very abilities that make them leaders are abilities that make them vulnerable. And of course nothing makes a person more susceptible to error than power. Even in small doses, power intoxicates; and in large doses it can be almost lethal to both the perpetrator and the victims.

When you see David react to the petulant and ill-advised message from Nabal, you see his future hanging in the balance. You see both the decisiveness necessary for leadership and the impetuosity than can ambush and destroy a leader. If you care about David's future, you pray that someone will lay a restraining hand on David's soul before he does something stupid.

Abigail fills this need with consummate insight. She realizes that David's ego has been offended. She had had enough experience with Nabal's foolishness to understand its shallowness and to feel the exquisite pain of its cut. She was equipped to feel David's pain. So it is that she dismounted and bowed to the dust before David. It was not an act of feigned humility; Abigail understood that she was dealing with a man with a badly damaged ego and she knew how to meet that need. She claimed blame for what had happened, when anyone could see that she had nothing to do with the crime. But her act of accepting the blame made clear that David bore no fault and diverted attention from the ugliness of the scene itself. Her generosity in seeking to accept the blame made Nabal's conduct all the more ridiculous and cast the whole incident in a very different light, thus defusing David's wrath.

Then Abigail reminded David that he was a called man, with a very large assignment just down the road. In doing so she put the Nabal incident in holy perspective. How foolish it would be for David, a prince by God's appointment no less, to bother with defending his ego for a wealthy but quite petty Nabal! It was an action beneath a person of David's character and future. Abigail's humility and her reasoned appeal reminded David of who he was, of the anointing Samuel had placed upon him so many years earlier. She reminded David that he was to have a place in history and that he must not mess it up. Thus she put the whole Nabal incident in logical and divine perspective.

She was right, of course, in warning David that if he "shed blood without cause" he would suffer "pangs of conscience" for the rest of his life. More than that, it could have derailed David's future. It could have made the hero of the battle with Goliath look like little more than a small-time hoodlum who had gone from military heroism to leading a gang of disenfranchised young men. If that happened, there would never be a King David.

Would to God that every national leader, every corporate executive, every star of entertainment or sports had an Abigail! Indeed, all of us need an Abigail at various occasions in our lives. Have you left some conversation and thought an hour later of some very clever rejoinder that you wish had come to you when the iron was hot? Me too. But I've come more and more to thank God my answer was slow in coming and to wish that I were more often less glib. I remember asking a church secretary one morning if a letter I had dictated the previous day was perhaps a little too strong. She answered, "It didn't really sound like you." She meant that it didn't sound like the kind of person I want to be—and I was sorry that I hadn't asked the secretary before I mailed the letter.

Life is full of consequences. Most of our conversations and actions are routine enough that the consequences prove to be inconsequential. But now and again we speak a word, write a letter, send an e-mail, make a decision, do a deed with ever widening circles of influence. And unfortunately, we don't always get a warning before such words or deeds are done. David must have made dozens if not hundreds of such in the years before he became king; the one with Nabal was a crucial one—and in the goodness of God, Abigail was there to save the day.

I suppose one long chapter in the Bible is all one could ask for a minor supporting character in the unfolding story of human redemption, but I can't help wishing there was more about Abigail. We learn that, like another wife, Ahinoam, she continued to travel with David in his work as a freelance soldier and security agent, and that in one instance she was taken captive in that perilous occupation. And I find great pleasure in seeing her with David as he becomes king, fulfilling the anointing that Samuel had placed on him almost a generation earlier.

I don't know what went through Abigail's mind at that coronation time or what David might have said to her. Perhaps he was too busy with kingship, with meetings and honorary delegations and such stuff of office. But I hope that somewhere in that busy first week of royal power David said, "Abigail, my dear, I will always remember the day you dismounted from a donkey and saved me from myself and my tender ego. It has something to do with our being here today, you know."

And Abigail answers, "Thank you, m'lord." And David hears the playful lilt in Abigail's word of honor.

CHAPTER ELEVEN

Counselor to Kings and Clergy

Scripture Reading: 2 Kings 22:3-20; 2 Chronicles 34:8-28

Perhaps I should begin this chapter with a disclaimer. A disclaimer, as you know, is the kind of statement that persons in certain positions issue in order to make clear that they are not speaking with personal prejudice in what they're about to say or write. I begin with such a statement just now because I realize that you may wonder why I have chosen to devote a chapter of this book to a biblical character you've perhaps not heard of before or who, at best, has never seemed to you to be a major biblical personality.

I am about to make such a statement, but before we're done with the story of the biblical woman named Huldah, I hope you will feel that she needs no justifying argument. With that said, I admit that I first looked with unique favor on the biblical Huldah because a very long time ago I knew, and was impressed by, one of her namesakes. Hulda Weintz was my sixth grade Sunday school teacher at the Helping Hand Mission (Methodist) in Sioux City, Iowa. Although I had a number of preachers and evangelists in my catalog of boyhood heroes, I came to some of my most important decisions through the guidance of Sunday school teachers. Hulda Weintz made several impressions on me, the most important of which was that she was my first financial advisor; specifically, she taught me to tithe. I have followed that practice ever since. Every year, when I make my pilgrimage through my hometown, I include among the schools, libraries, and churches of my childhood the exceedingly modest home where Hulda and her sister Caroline (neither one ever married) lived when I was a boy. Come to think of it, theirs is the only home on my pilgrimage route except for the several homes in which our family lived through those years and the home of a boyhood friend who remained a friend through all of his life.

Now that I have cleared my soul of a possible prejudice, let me tell you the story of the extraordinary woman of ancient times named Huldah. At the point of her entrance into sacred history the times were neither the best nor the worst that her nation had ever known. Let's just say that they were uncertain. For fifty-five years Manasseh had reigned over Judah. Much of that time he had been a man of sin, but later he humbled himself and became an exemplary man and a fine king. Apparently, however, he did not reform in time to affect his son Amon redemptively. In the end, of course, we all decide for ourselves what kind of persons we will be, and while the odds are decidedly tilted by the lives and teachings of others, the final vote in our destiny is our own. The biblical chronicler writes that Amon "did not humble himself before the LORD, as his father Manasseh had humbled himself, but this Amon incurred more and more guilt" (2 Chronicles 33:23). His servants conspired in his assassination after Amon had been on the throne only two years.

The immediate heir to the throne was an eight-year-old boy, Josiah. In the ancient world of kings and queens, this sort of thing didn't seem to cause the kind of havoc we would expect. While a king's power was absolute, most of the day-by-day administration was in the hands of a variety of royal servants. The real question was how a young king would respond once he was old enough to realize the extent of his power and would decide how he would use it.

In Josiah's case, it was a happy story. Here's how the Bible puts it: "In the eighth year of his reign, while he was still a boy, he began to seek the God of his ancestor David, and in the twelfth year he began to purge Judah and Jerusalem" with a series of vigorous reforms (34:3). I wish I knew what went on in Josiah's life in those four years when he was "still a boy" of sixteen and began to seek God and when at twenty he became a reformer, leading his nation back to God. I wonder who his counselors were, if any, and how it is that he was so deeply changed.

One's wonder is all the greater when we read what happened next, because we learn that at this time the nation apparently had no written scripture immediately at hand. We can only judge that Josiah was getting his spiritual direction by what others were telling him and by way of his personal communion with God.

It was enough, in fact, that he cleared away many of the pagan altars and practices that had come to dominate Judah's worship, but eventually he began "to repair the house of the LORD his God" (34:8). In the process of this cleaning and remodeling, an astonishing thing happened: "the priest Hilkiah found the book of the law of the LORD given through Moses" (34:14)—most likely the book of Deuteronomy.

Let me interrupt the Huldah story even before we get to her to raise a question: how did the scriptures get lost in the house of the Lord? My answer: where else would they get lost, except in the place responsible for their care? In the midst of all of the clamor about the Bible in public schools and plaques

with the Ten Commandments in government buildings, I submit that you can have such semblances of religion and still lose
the word of God if those who are most responsible for it—the
church and the people of God—allow it to lose its authority
and power within the temple.

But back to our story and to Huldah. The priest,
Hilkiah, hardly knew what to do when he discovered the
dust-covered documents of Judah's faith. He was wise
enough, however, to know that he dare not redeposit the
documents in the dust. He took it to "the secretary
Shaphan," an organizational official within the priesthood,
who then brought it to the king, and furthermore, "read it
aloud to the king" (34:18).

When the king heard the reading, "he tore his clothes"
(34:19). Of all the good things that can be said for King
Josiah, perhaps this is the greatest. Josiah was so serious
about following God that he realized how far short he and
his nation were from the full purposes of God. He might
easily have rested on the admirable and courageous reforms
he had already instituted. He might, in fact, have heard the
words of Deuteronomy and have congratulated himself on
how much he had done to bring his nation into a better
relationship with the Almighty. Instead, in holy fear, he tore
his regal garments. Here was a leader, indeed: a person who
led repentance by being the first to repent. It's always easier,
you know, to preach or to recommend repentance than to
practice it.

But now, what to do? Where to begin? If the supreme political leader, the king, and the key religious leader, Hilkiah the priest, already have the document, where do you turn? Logically, it looks as if you've gone about as far as you can go. If this had happened in seventeenth-century England, with the King of England and the Archbishop of Canterbury at such a crisis, where would they have turned? I suspect they would have looked at each other and concluded that the problem was in their hands because there was no place beyond them to go.

But the priest Hilkiah and King Josiah had a solution: "they went to the prophet Huldah, the wife of Shallum son of Tokhath son of Hasrah, keeper of the wardrobe (who lived in Jerusalem in the Second Quarter)" (34:22). I give you the full quotation, including some data that may seem incidental, including the husband's family line, his office (which seems that of an ordinary public servant), where they lived, and where in Jerusalem that happened to be because I want you to know everything we really know about Huldah. And as you can see, it isn't much.

But clearly, obviously, dramatically, Huldah is a woman of distinction and of acknowledged parts. At a time like this, the political-religious leadership of an officially religious country doesn't turn to a nonentity. This is no time for a novice, no time for learning on the job. We turn now to a recognized leader. There is no evidence that Huldah is someone in a list of prospects or that they had a choice

before her or a back-up if she didn't come through. Huldah
is *it*. As we used to say in our old high school sports cheer,
"if she can't do it, nobody can."

So who is Huldah? Logic teaches us that when there is
an effect (or a result) there must be a cause behind the
effect, and the larger the effect, the greater the cause behind
it. This relationship of cause and effect is easier to trace in
physical matters than in human beings. Nevertheless we
look for the link in humans. When we see some particularly
successful person, we begin looking at his or her ancestry,
education, andparticular talents in order to understand his
or her greatness. Some searches seem quite obvious: the
person has strong family stock, comes under the influence
of great teachers, and is associated with favorable circumstances. Other instances, however, are more difficult to
explain. One thinks of Abraham Lincoln: what cause in his
family line, education, or favorable circumstances produced
the effect that produced the president, emancipator, and
master of communication?

So how is it with the woman Huldah? We have a record
of only this one incident from her career, but we have it
because she was already a person of reputation and
achievement within her nation. In this instance she spoke
with clarity, assurance, and persuasiveness, but how is it
that established leaders in religion and statecraft turned to
her for assistance?

I hardly need to tell you that all the odds were against

Huldah. To be a woman in her day was primarily to be the carrier of life from one generation to the next. For matters of leadership in home, business, politics, and religion, people turned instinctively to men. Yet at a time in Judah's history that the leaders recognized as a watershed, the king and his advisors turned without hesitancy to a woman, Huldah. Her reputation was such that her name was the first and apparently the only one to come to mind.

And what was it exactly that brought Huldah to mind? It was the king's command,

> Go, inquire of the LORD for me, for the people, and for all Judah, concerning the words of this book that has been found; for great is the wrath of the LORD that is kindled against us, because our ancestors did not obey the words of this book, to do according to all that is written concerning us. (2 Kings 22:12-13)

Huldah had a reputation for her walk with God. When the king ordered his advisors to "inquire of the LORD" they went directly to Huldah. It was their perception that the shortest and surest way to know the mind of God was to talk with the prophetess Huldah.

This is a singular reputation, indeed. The nineteenth-century Scottish historian and philosopher, Thomas Carlyle, is reported to have said that what his village needed was a pastor who knew God by more than hearsay. I suspect that many preachers are in the "hearsay" category; they are more comfortable quoting the faith of others than declaring their own. In the days of King Josiah there were thousands of ordained clergy in the land; this was the role of the tribe of Levi. But when the king wanted someone to "inquire of the Lord," the Levitical leaders beat a path to Jerusalem's second quarter, to the home of Huldah and Shallum.

How did Huldah get such a reputation? Purely and simply, by the integrity and purity of her faith. Apparently her family was of no special significance; the biblical writer tells us of her husband's father and grandfather but nothing of her ancestry. She had no academic degrees. There's no hint that she had some ancient equivalent of a television ministry. Somehow she had become known as a prophet, as a person whose walk with God was so consistent and so empowered that to meet her was to sense that one was in the presence of a person who walked with God.

I have known such persons. If there is any good in me it is primarily because such people have touched my life. Since I have known such persons I should be able to describe Huldah, but I can't. Some have been women and some men. Some have been old whereas a few have been young. Some have had only the most modest education whereas others have been learned. Nearly all of them laughed easily and also came to tears when they saw pain in others. None of them were self-impressed. This is probably a key issue: I suspect that when others tell you that you are special, you may easily come to believe it. It is when you begin to believe it, that you begin to lose it.

I believe that people like Huldah are called by God, but I doubt that they know the unique quality of their calling. I believe, too, that more receive Huldah's call than fulfill it. That is, I'm very sure that God has intended for more of us to become persons of whom others can "inquire of the LORD" but fail to fulfill God's gracious intention. I believe that people like Huldah are the salt of the earth and that it is to the degree that they are among us that our world is saved from destruction by its own self-corruption.

So a delegation of five men, headed by the priest Hilkiah, came to the home of Huldah with a message from the king. These were men of dignity and influence, and they were representing the king, a very good king, at that. Yet they came with true humility, recognizing that with all of their official power they needed the help of a woman who had essentially no conventional significance. We have no description of her home or of her person. Clearly, the Bible sees no importance in the details, else they would be part of the story.

We have no record of how the delegation presented their cause and nothing of how Huldah heard them. They had come to her for a word from the Lord, and she answered in kind: "Thus says the LORD, the God of Israel: Tell the man who sent you to me" (2 Kings 22:15)—and with that, I pause. Huldah calls Josiah "the man," not "the king" or "his royal highness" or any other distinguishing name or title; he is simply "the man who sent you to me."

The ground is level at the altar of God. All persons kneel at the same elevation, though I think that some are so wise as to wonder that others are not higher than they are. Later Huldah will refer to "the man" as the King of Judah, but as a basic inquirer, he is like any other person.

Huldah's message was severe. Yes, the judgment of God would come, as predicted in the book of the Law because the nation had forsaken God's purposes. God's wrath would come and "not be quenched" (22:17). As I read the Scriptures I sense that the judgments of God usually come by way of the world of politics and economics, and once these wheels begin turning they continue to their end. But Huldah had a word of mercy. Because King Josiah "was penitent" and because he "humbled himself before the Lord," he would "not see all the disaster" (22:19-20) that would come to Jerusalem.

We hear no more of Huldah. I'm sure many people, common and exalted, continued to seek her out. I think she would object that I describe her as "counselor to kings and clergy." She was a prophet of God, and people knew it without her hanging a sign over her door or printing professional cards. If you wanted to "inquire of God" and wanted help from someone you sensed was somehow closer to God than the rest of us mortals, you went to her.

I'm glad the spiritual descendants of Huldah are still present in our world. I thank God for those who have been part of my life. I pray that you know some Huldah too.

CHAPTER TWELVE

Two Young Women of Courage

Scripture Reading: Esther 4:10-17; 2 Kings 5:1-19

This is the story of two young women. One was a queen; her name is with us still in the title of a book of the Bible and in thousands of women around the world who continue to bear her name. She is a legendary figure with the Jewish people; they celebrate her story each year in the holiday Purim. Her physical beauty is the stuff of poetry and paintings. *The Oxford Dictionary of Quotations* carries her most famous sentence, a line that many no doubt recite without knowing its origin.

The other young woman is anonymous; she was a slave girl. We know nothing of her physical appearance, which isn't surprising since it's difficult for a serving girl to look like a fashion model. The Bible records one brief speech made up of two even shorter sentences. I suspect that someone, somewhere, sometime—an unknown novelist or poet perhaps, and very likely a preacher or Sunday school teacher—has quoted the young servant girl, but not in a way that has found its place in the esteemed literature of our world.

The two young women had several things in common, however. Both were Jewish and both were far from home. As far as we know, one of them never saw her native land, the land of her ancestors, and the other one, kidnapped in time of war, almost surely never had opportunity to return to her homeland. Both were women of faith, and both came to a place of very great peril where their very lives were in danger—although perhaps the slave girl never realized it. And both were women of exemplary courage.

Let's talk first about the legendary figure, the woman Esther. A generation or two earlier the Babylonians had invaded Judah, conquered the land, and taken captive the best and the brightest and the ablest of the Jews. Later the Medes and Persians had conquered the Babylonians, and Esther's family and the other Jewish captives were now subject to the newly dominant empire. We know little about the day-by-day lives of Esther and her neighbors except that they were in an inferior position as an alien people and though some of them were in settings of comfort they were always in danger of some outbreak of prejudice and violence. On the whole, therefore, they learned to present a low profile and to maintain a manner of wise amiability.

The story in the biblical Book of Esther begins in a world far removed from the daily life of the immigrant population of Jews—with a description, in fact, of the size and grandeur of the empire of the Medes and Persians and of the excess with which the king, Ahasuerus, paraded his nation's power. For one hundred eighty days, Ahasuerus "displayed the great wealth of his kingdom and the splendour and pomp of his majesty" (Esther 1:4). But what can a king do after showing off endless (and eventually tedious) displays of jewelry and artifacts, raiding the royal wine cellar for new variety, and pushing to the limits the skills of an army of chefs? What now can he do to impress his guests? (And by the way, how sad is it for a king to feel it necessary to impress other people? What value in being a king if your ego so desperately needs outside approval?)

Following the rule that nothing succeeds like excess, the king chose to boast by way of humiliating another, and who better to use for this than his proudest possession: Queen Vashti. He would "show the peoples and the officials her beauty; for she was fair to behold" (1:11). But the queen had a mind of her own. She was not only accustomed to living like a queen but also, I suspect, had a fine sense of contempt for the sycophants whom the king was so anxious to impress. Indeed, she may also have had some contempt for the king himself.

So Vashti refused to acquiesce to the king's request and the king deposed her as queen. He then issued a national decree "proclaimed throughout all his kingdom, vast as it was, all women will give honour to their husbands, high and low alike" (1:20). When his anger abated and he realized that he was without a queen, he received counsel from his servants. They recommended a national beauty contest of the fairest virgins in the land, with the winner replacing Queen Vashti. "This pleased the king, and he did so" (2:4).

Only now do we meet Esther. She is Jewish and an orphan. Her cousin Mordecai has raised her since her parents' death and has adopted her; "and the girl was fair and beautiful" (2:7). In the midst of all the beautiful young women in an empire that reached more than 127 provinces from India to Ethiopia, this girl of the ghetto stood out. I think it is fair to conclude that she possessed the kind of indefinable attractiveness that we refer to as "inner beauty." After all, there are only so many ways to measure the contours of a face, the linearity of a form, the luster of the eye, and the texture of hair and skin; eventually one turns to something beyond measure: the person. Esther had such unique quality that she "was admired by all who saw her," and "the king loved Esther more than all the other women" that were brought before him (2:15, 17).

There are many details in this story that I can't take the

time to discuss, so I urge you to read the book of Esther for yourself. Let me summarize by saying that there is always someone in the king's court (or the president's cabinet or the corporate headquarters) who wants still more power, and there was such a man in Ahasuerus's inner circle, a man named Haman. He was carefully and steadily moving up in the ranks but his pleasure was diminished daily by a rather obscure citizen who refused to kowtow to him. This difficult personality happened to be Mordecai, Esther's cousin. Haman concluded that no honor would satisfy him as long as this one man continued to ignore him. Still, Haman felt it was beneath him to destroy one insignificant person, so when he learned that Haman was a Jew, a member of a relatively small but significant immigrant people, he persuaded the king to sign a document destroying all Jews on a particular date. The king didn't know that his fair Esther was herself a Jewish alien, and Esther didn't know that the edict had been issued.

But Mordecai knew, and he sent word to Esther, along with an appeal that she speak to the king without delay. But this was not easy to do. A king is a king, and kings and other such persons often become prickly about their authority. If anyone in the king's court came to see the king without being called, they were put to death. When Esther, by way of a messenger, explained this deadly protocol to Mordecai, he immediately replied,

Do not think that in the king's palace you will escape any
more than all the other Jews. For if you keep silence at such
a time as this, relief and deliverance will rise for the Jews
from another quarter, but you and your father's family will
perish. Who knows? Perhaps you have come to royal dignity for just such a time as this. (4:13-14)

When the person who has adopted and raised you talks
like that, you listen, and probably you draw upon some of
the strength that person invested in you. Esther sent word to
Mordecai to gather all the Jews in Susa to hold a three-day
fast on her behalf, as she and her maids would do, and then
she would go to the king, "though it is against the law."
Esther concluded her message with her signature phrase:
"and if I perish, I perish" (4:16). That, indeed, is courage.

The rest, as they say, is history. It is also myth, poetry, leg-
end, and song. The king granted Esther an audience, though
she hadn't been in his presence for more than a month. In a
dramatically choreographed plan, Esther made her appeal to
the king, and she won. Not only did King Ahasuerus send out
an edict countermanding his earlier document, he also ordered
the execution of Haman, whom he recognized as a dangerous
person to have in his body of advisors.

As for Esther, classic playwrights and composers have
told her story: Lope de Vega for the Spanish, Racine for the
French, and Handel in an oratorio. The world Jewish community celebrates her story annually in the Feast of Purim,
and "at least twenty-five Jewish communities throughout
the world observe their own particular 'Purim,' recalling, in

ceremonies similar to the Purim celebration, their own unique deliverance from a tyrant."[1] And of course Hadassah, the worldwide Jewish women's organization, takes its name from Esther's Hebrew name.

It is easy to lose my second story in the shade of Esther. I refuse to do so. As it happens, however, it is easy to lose our second heroine's story in the account itself, because we don't have her name and she isn't the lead character. Nevertheless, without her there wouldn't be a story.

It happened this way. In the days when the prophet Elisha was contesting for the soul of the nation of Israel, as his mentor Elijah had done before him, there was a military hero in the land of Aram (Syria): Naaman. He was "a great man and in high favour with his master, because by him the LORD had given victory to Aram" (2 Kings 5:1).

This is one of the few instances in the Old Testament where we read that God is specifically at work in the activities of nations other than Israel or Judah. In this case the Bible doesn't tell us why God chose to bless this general, and we have no idea whether the general sensed that he was enjoying God's favor. As the story unfolds, however, we realize that this general was spiritually hungry (though he probably wouldn't have analyzed himself that way). We do learn early that General Naaman's public success was blighted by private tragedy. The Bible puts it succinctly: "The man, though a mighty warrior, suffered from leprosy" (5:1).

As a term, ancient leprosy covered several skin diseases ranging from minor and sometimes temporary disorders to what we now call Hansen's Disease. But because in those days it was difficult if not impossible to diagnose the progress of the disease, people feared contact with the afflicted. Their fear is perhaps not that different from the precautions that millions of people took a few years ago when there was an outbreak of pulmonary disorders internationally. Many were unsure which illnesses were routine and which possibly deadly, so hundreds of thousands of city dwellers donned protective face masks.

We don't know the degree or severity of Naaman's disease. Because of his prominence and his importance as a military leader, society no doubt gave him more latitude. Whatever the degree of his disease, it was clearly a matter of enormous concern because eventually it would bring an end to his military leadership. Without a doubt Naaman and his king had exhausted all the medical skills of Aram and all of the "magic" that may have been practiced in the land at that time. Nothing had availed. I suppose that in those days, as today, people spoke of Naaman as a "hopeless case."

When I was a boy I often heard adults conclude a quiet discussion with the sentence, "Well, man's extremity is God's opportunity." I have since learned that this little proverb has been part of our human wisdom since the early seventeenth century, but I'm sure it is older than that. In one form or another it is as old as faith itself. The fascinating part in our faith stories, however, is how God finds such doors of opportunity. In Naaman's story, as in many that you and I have known, the door of entry was a modest one, one not at all likely for the world of kings and generals. Here's how the Bible tells it: "Now the Arameans on one of their raids had taken a young girl captive from the land of Israel, and she served Naaman's wife" (2 Kings 5:2).

When we're talking with someone who is passing through one of life's dark and lonely places, we sometimes say, "I feel for you. I can imagine what you're going through." At this point in our story, I want to disclaim that sentence. I simply can't imagine what the girl from Israel was going through. I've had some hard times in my life (many of which I've brought on myself and all of which have done me good), but I can't imagine what it would be like, as a child or a teenager, to be taken captive by an enemy army, carried to a foreign land, and pressed into involuntary service with no prospect of ever again seeing homeland, friends, or family. I cannot imagine it.

I can imagine, however, saying what I've heard people say hundreds of times as they have told me of their sorrows: "I can't see why this had to happen to me." Most of us have the idea that we ought to be exempt from life's misfortunes. If the "young girl from the land of Israel" had such feelings, she must have gotten over them in good time. I can also imagine how, under such circumstances, I might try carefully to avoid offending my employers (or to use a more precise word, my owners, for she was a slave, a captive in a foreign land).

But this young woman was quite fearless. I suspect that some would say that she lacked common sense. As maid to Naaman's wife, she knew what the family was going through. She became a partner in their pain. So one day "she said to her mistress, 'If only my lord were with the prophet who is in Samaria! He would cure him of his leprosy'" (5:3).

Her message was impolitic and daring. It isn't wise for a captive to tell the captors that his or her homeland has something the captors don't have. But far worse, if your captors take your counsel seriously and it proves unsuccessful, quite surely you will become *persona non grata*. For people to spend a small fortune and days of difficult travel only to come home disappointed . . . well, the young woman was taking quite a chance.

Her owners took her seriously. Obviously, they had come to trust her. They could see that her words were a sincere expression of love and concern. Something in her manner convinced them that there was a basis for her belief in this unknown prophet. And of course they were at that point of despair where they were willing to try almost anything.

What followed was for a while a comedy of errors. When Naaman told his king "what the girl from the land of Israel had said" (5:4), the king did what kings and executives do: he went to work at the executive level, by sending a message to the king of Israel. Naaman arrived at the king's palace with his retinue and the message, "'When this letter reaches you, know that I have sent to you my servant Naaman, that you may cure him of his leprosy'" (5:6). The king of Israel "tore his clothes," figuring that the king of Aram was "trying to pick a quarrel" (5:7).

Word got to Elisha the prophet, who promptly sent word, "Let him come to me, that he may learn that there is a prophet in Israel" (5:8). When Naaman's grand procession reached Elisha's house, the prophet didn't even come to the door. He sent a preemptory message: go and bathe in the River Jordan seven times. Naaman was in big trouble. He had come a long way, at great expense and at royal order, and he expected a medical counselor with a better bedside manner. He announced that if he wanted a bath, they had better rivers back in Syria.

Power often seems to diminish common sense. This is why people with power need to have some people around them who are without power. One of Naaman's servants dared to offer common sense: If the prophet had told you to do a great thing, you would do it. Why not try what the prophet has recommended? Naaman was smart enough to take the advice, and he was healed of his leprosy. Still more, he was converted. He returned to his homeland a devout believer in the God of Israel.

And that's pretty much the story of the Israelite slave girl. The Bible doesn't tell us that her employers rewarded her with freedom or with better living quarters. We know nothing more of what happened to her. I insist that if Elisha's counsel had not brought healing to her master, she might easily have lost her life; life was cheap for slaves taken in battle. But through her courage, health and joy came to the people she served, and her employer came to faith in God. What is the value of one soul?

I know that the slave girl's story is not as glamorous as Esther's, and I know that there is no Jewish holiday celebrating her deeds, and no woman's organization named in her honor, especially since no one knows her name. But I submit that her courage and her faith were of a piece with Esther's. That's why I decided to tell their stories together. They were in different times, places, and positions, but they were both great women. And I submit that we should measure greatness not by some isolated standard of wealth, headlines, or historic memory, but by our doing the right thing at the right time in the place where God entrusts us to live and to serve.

This is where courage finds its measure. Not by life in the abstract and not by some philosophical code, but by integrity where opportunity or destiny thrust decision upon us. We come to such human junctures more often than other people know, and sometimes more than we ourselves realize. For ours is a world where courage is needed in doses large, average, and insignificant. But whatever the hour, the call is divine. By God's help, the courage will be right for the hour. And by God's grace, we will rise up and claim it.

Study Guide
Suggestions for Leading a Study of
A Faith of Her Own

Shannon Sumrall

This study guide is designed to enhance your experience of *A Faith of Her Own* by assisting you in your reflection and discussion of the book. The discussion guide is grouped into sections by chapter. In each chapter section you will find a brief summary of the chapter, reflection/discussion questions, and a prayer focus pertaining to that particular woman of faith.

The reflection/discussion questions will guide you in examining the lives of these women of the Old Testament and determining how their characteristics are embodied in the women around us. Women are relational beings, and these questions are designed both to help us remember women who have blessed us in relationship and to inspire us to bless others in relationship with the Lord.

The prayer focus sections include prayers of petition or thanksgiving to the Lord, as well as interactive prayer activities. Colossians 4:2 reads, "Devote yourselves to prayer, keeping alert in it with thanksgiving." In this context, our whole lives can be an opportunity for prayer. A conversation, a move to action, an artistic creation, a remembrance, a word of praise, a testimony of a life lived well all can constitute prayer. It is also important to note that our prayers can be offered both with others and alone.

The hope is that the materials offered in this study guide, together with your own reflection and insights from your reading, will be a reminder that we are all needed in the body of Christ. As Ephesians 4:11-13 tells us,

> The gifts he gave were that some would be apostles, some prophets, some evangelists, some pastors and teachers, to equip the saints for the work of ministry, for building up the body of Christ, until all of us come to the unity of the faith and of the knowledge of the Son of God, to maturity, to the measure of the full stature of Christ.

Suggestions for Group Study Leaders

Remember that every group is unique. Talk with the members of your group to determine a pace and approach to reading and study that feels comfortable and appropriate for all. Give yourself permission to modify and adapt the format of this study as it suits your group's needs.

Help ensure that your group will be a safe place to share. Emphasize the importance of mutual respect and confidentiality. Let all group members have an equal opportunity to participate. Look for ways to get everyone involved while respecting the fact that each person has a different comfort zone.

Allowing time during your group meeting to share prayer requests and to pray for and with one another can be a valuable part of the study and may help you bring it from the "head" level to the "heart" level. Providing food and beverages as snacks or as a meal can be an asset to fellowship, and designating a certain week where the group engages in a special planned activity together may provide an opportunity for fellowship and spiritual growth as well. Encourage group members to interact with the chapter material through activities such as independent research, journaling, painting, creating a collage, or online dialogue before your group comes together each week. These sorts of activities can be shared among group members or may be done individually as a means of personal growth and reflection.

Above all, sit and listen for the Lord's direction. God will lead and guide you and your group, perhaps in ways that are unexpected. Enjoy the journey!

Suggestions for Participants

Remember that you bring a unique perspective and experience, and your group would not be complete without your presence. Remember to read through the chapter material before the group meeting and look for ways to interact with it. This can be done through independent research, journaling, online dialogue, creating original works of art, and many other ways. The important thing is to record your thoughts and to interact with the subject matter. In addition to your own learning, this kind of interactive study can help you bring a greater depth to the group experience.

If you do not have an opportunity to read the chapter material before your group meeting, there are still ways to be involved and to share in the journey with others. The prayer is that through this study you will find yourself closer to the heart of the Lord and to being the person God has made you to be. This study is a celebration of women of the Old Testament, as well as the women of today. May it be a joyful journey!

Chapter 1
The Ultimate First Lady

Chapter Summary

This chapter gives insight into Eve, the first woman, a person who chose to hold onto grace and hope rather than focusing on her losses and the consequences of her sin.

Reflection/Discussion Questions

1. What comes to mind when you hear the term *First Lady*?
2. What were the descriptions of woman and of the role she was created to fill?
3. Describe your response to being created in God's image and the intentionality behind it.
4. Remember back to one of the most perfect gifts you have ever received and your thoughts and feelings upon receiving it. What do you think happened in Adam when he woke up and saw Eve?
5. One of Eve's greatest strengths turned into a place that got her into trouble. What is a strength of yours that you have seen lead you to places you never meant to go?
6. Eve didn't recognize she needed God's help until it was too late. We, living in the aftermath of her choices, know we need it. Where can you go today and ask for help in a situation that has you in waters that are beyond your depth?

7. Our tendency can be to hold ourselves hostage to our past choices when the Lord wants to offer mercy and grace. Is there a place that you are identifying yourself by the person you used to be? What is one step you can take toward freedom today?

8. From the youngest in our race to the oldest among us, blaming is something we've embraced. Give an example of when you blamed someone else rather than owning up to your actions.

9. Adam chose not to identify Eve for her past, but to help her lay hold of her future. Tell of a person who has been that voice for you, and tell of something he or she might have said to help you believe him or her.

10. Eve had no idea that the consequences of her sin would affect her children so fully and deeply. Where do you still need to receive grace for the consequences of your choices?

11. Take some time as a group to pray about the future the Lord has in store then pray as a group for help in getting our hopes and dreams up to God's level.

Prayer Focus

We have the magnificent privilege that Adam and Eve did not share in. We know the term repent. Repentance means to turn and go the other direction. We can ask for forgiveness, find cleansing from our pasts, and step into the truth of who we are—grace givers and hope bearers who call on the name of the Lord.

Dear God, we are part of the "resounding success" of your creation. Would you show us the places where we have chosen to listen to misguided voices and give us the strength to repent? Help us, please, live in the truth of who we are and operate in authenticity, thus making a way for others to experience grace and freedom as well.

Chapter 2
A Woman Who Married Trouble

Chapter Summary

In this chapter, we hear of Cain's wife, who, whether or not she knew what she was getting into, found herself in the painful place of hoping for a prince when she'd been given a frog.

Reflection/Discussion Questions

1. Have you ever read this story and thought about the wife of Cain?

2. What was your immediate response when you read about her? Pity? Understanding? Gratitude it wasn't you? Something else?

3. It is often in the most difficult relationships in our lives that the greatest work is done in us. Where is a place you have been fighting the work the Lord wants to do in you because you can only focus on what you want done in someone else?

4. Who is the man or woman who comes to mind when reading this? your spouse? child? sibling? coworker? friend?

5. The pain and weight that we carry on behalf of others can be paralyzing at times and something Jesus never meant for us to take on. Are you willing to hand this person over to Jesus, the only one who can redeem

what may seem to be a lost cause? If your response is no, will you take a moment and ask why?

6. Take a moment and ask the Lord for a deep under-standing that this dear one was created in the image of God and ask for a heavenly perspective.

7. Though it may be out of your comfort zone, picture Jesus standing beside the cross. Will you walk this loved one over to Jesus and leave him to Jesus?

8. The God who never slumbers or sleeps has a stunning plan for this loved one and will continue to fight to make that plan a reality. It's not all up to you! What does that evoke in you?

9. Our resources aren't enough and were never meant to be. Will you allow the God of love and hope to fill you on behalf of the one for whom your heart is breaking?

10. What is one way this week that you can speak life and encouragement to the one your heart is breaking for?

11. Our becoming who we were made to be can be the biggest blessing we can offer to those around us. What is one step you can take this week to become who you were made to be?

Prayer Focus

This wife of Cain found herself in a position that she might not have chosen had she known the whole picture. Humans grow and change, and we have no way of seeing the whole picture. We have a God who does, who knows us and those we dream for inside and out. What does it mean to embrace the calling on our lives to love regardless of the outcome? We can only do that with God's strength and heart, and the Lord longs to come to our aid if we only ask.

Dear God, you have given me the gift of being in the lives of people who have not yet seen the life you created them for. Show me, please, how to be one who speaks life and possibility and hope for them and never, ever, ever gives up.

Chapter 3
The Compleat Woman

Chapter Summary

This chapter introduces us to Sarah, who finds herself in a seemingly hopeless and impossible position. But such circumstances are often the best opportunity to find the grace and power of God.

Reflection/Discussion Questions

1. What do you remember about the story of Abraham and Sarah?
2. Sarah would have been known in her culture as a childless woman. It was part of her life, but in that era it would have been the primary definition. How would you define yourself?
3. The author broadened the definition of leadership in this chapter. How does that affect the way you view your life?
4. We have all been given influence in the lives of people around us. Who do you have influence with, and what does that influence look like?
5. Who are the people whom God has given you to follow? Do you (as recommended in Hebrews 13:17) make it a joy for them to lead you?
6. Whose faith has made a way for you to be who you are today? Whose firsthand faith has influenced you greatly?

7. Who do you support by secondhand faith?

8. Despite the longer life spans in those days, humanly speaking, Sarah having children was impossible. Describe a place that seems impossible in your life.

9. Tell of a time in your life when you took matters into your own hands and the consequences you ended up paying.

10. Being childless was a part of Sarah's reality but not a part of her destiny. What has God spoken about your destiny that you need hope for today?

11. Sarah went from laughter to a place of solid belief in the Lord's promises. Would you take a moment and ask God for the grace to stand in a place of solid belief?

Prayer Focus

Although Abraham and Sarah had not adapted the cultural way of providing children, after they heard the promise from God, Sarah decided to take matters into her own hands. Our great God, once a promise has been made, will provide the means to make that promise a reality. We need only wait and listen for marching orders. Christine Caine says, "God's appointed time is different than our due date." Where do you need to let the Lord redefine your waiting?

Holy and joyous God, nothing is impossible with you. Would you please give me eyes to see beyond the current circumstances and reality into the destiny that you have dreamed? Give me courage to wait when I need to wait and to act when I need to act. Lead on, Great God.

Chapter 4
A Mother Who Played Favorites

Chapter Summary

This chapter gives insight into a woman God trusted to help the divine plan come to pass. It also explores some of the consequences of her choices after she manipulated circumstances to make the plan happen in her own way.

Reflection/Discussion Questions

1. When Rebekah met Abraham's servant, she was ready at that moment to serve, to run, and to pour, without a thought for herself or her agenda. How do you respond to interruptions, big or small?

2. Rebekah's response to the question of her willingness to go was decisive and seemed instantaneous. Tell of a time when your obedience to a step from the Lord came that effortlessly.

3. Helen Musick says, "Obedience brings blessing." Where have you seen that to be true in your own life?

4. If there is a next step of obedience you haven't taken? What is a step in that direction you can take right now?

5. To our knowledge, Rebekah knew nothing of the prophecy or destiny of her family until she arrived in her home. Why do you think in some circumstances the Lord only tells us a little at a time?

6. Rebekah became pregnant as a result of prayer and received the prophecy as a result of prayer as well. Sometimes action will only happen as a result of prayer. God has incredible things to say to us and do through us, if we only stop and listen. How do you do at stopping to listen to the Lord in your life?

7. What keeps you from stopping to listen? What can you implement to help make listening more of a part of your life?

8. The Lord so often chooses to work outside the conventional way to accomplish specific purposes. What could be some of the reasons for doing this?

9. Have you ever exchanged something precious because you were blinded by the immediate? What would you tell that younger version of yourself today?

10. Rebekah didn't complain to the Lord; she inquired. In what area(s) of your life do you need to take time to inquire today?

11. Rebekah was chosen to guard and help the plan of the Lord happen in her day, and although she didn't do it perfectly, she did it. What has God called you to do in your day? What dreams has our God spoken to you? What step can you take today to further God's dreams for you?

Prayer Focus

Remembering God's faithfulness during our obedience can give us the courage to trust for our next steps. Where

do you need to cry out to God and then wait for a
response? The Lord wants to hear what you have to say, to
answer, and be in dialogue with you. God wants not only
to give us direction but also to walk with us through the
whole process.

*Lord God, you long to hear from me and you will
answer. Lord, I specifically need to hear from you. What do
you have to say to me in this area? Please give me the
patience to wait to hear and then the courage to act upon
your direction.*

Chapter 5
They May Have Been Twins—but Not Identical

Chapter Summary

Leah and Rachel were sisters who shared a husband but seemed to have had very little else in common. In circumstances that we are hard-pressed to understand, the Lord worked a plan that enabled them both to be ancestors who brought about and preserved God's people and, ultimately, the redemption plan for all humankind.

Reflection/Discussion Questions

1. In this section, we finally see Isaac fully acknowledging that Jacob was God's choice. From Isaac's grief, the Lord was able to speak the plan for his boy. How have you seen grief be an instrument that enables us to hear our God speak more clearly?

2. Jacob is now the possessor of the birthright: the blessing and the promise of the Covenant that he would be part of the line to help God's promise come to pass. What do you think was going through his mind on his seventeen-day trip?

3. We know that Jacob loved Rachel, but we don't hear that she loved him back. Do you wonder, perhaps, if she resented Leah being given in marriage first?

4. Leah names several of her children hoping they will bring the love of her husband, and we don't see that

she ever gets it. What promises do you cling to when things aren't as you would have planned them to be?

5. Leah could have chosen bitterness and resentment, and our human side wouldn't fault her for that. Do you think it was a one-time choice? How does one choose to not be overrun with the darkness?

6. Leah acknowledged that God's eyes were on her. The Lord watches over our lives and over our coming and going (as Psalm 121 tells us). How can that be a comfort to us in the midst of difficult circumstances?

7. Have you ever been loved only for your usefulness? What did that do to your heart, your sense of self-worth?

8. An everlasting love is the description (in Jeremiah 31) of God's love for us. We were loved before we were created, born, or ever did anything. Describe your response to this love.

9. There is a progression in Leah's child-naming. Judah, the fourth, means "this time I will praise the Lord." Where can you choose to praise God today?

10. The evidence of Leah's life pointed to a deep faith in the God who had promised a people as numerous as the sand on the seashore. What does having a personal faith mean for you in places where you are waiting for growth, waiting on a promise, waiting on people, waiting on God?

11. Rachel's choices point to envy, stealing, and manipulating to bring about what she thought she deserved. And in the middle of this, she has Joseph, who was chosen by God to rescue the Israelites in Egypt. Where have you seen God's redemptive work in the midst of your poor choices?

Prayer Focus

Leah found herself in the odd place of being her husband's second choice but God's first choice to carry the lineage of our Lord Jesus. She had no idea, but she chose to trust and praise anyway. Restoration is one of our God's specialties, and bringing beauty from ashes is a promise that is made to all who choose to place their trust in the Lord of heaven and earth. Where is there a place of pain or sorrow that could use a touch of the grace of God? What if you asked for the holy purpose of heaven to be brought about in your most difficult circumstances?

Gracious God, only you can fulfill the deepest longings of our hearts, and I find myself in a place of need. Please, Lord, help me trust you in this place. I choose to praise you and to give this to you, and I ask you to open to my eyes to your redemptive work in my life.

Chapter 6
The Original Big Sister

Chapter Summary

This chapter brings us Miriam, a big sister whose courage and leadership led to the exodus of the Israelites and who also exemplified the consequences of speaking against God's appointed leader.

Reflection/Discussion Questions

1. How many big sisters are in the room? How many had a big sister? If you had a memory sparked during this lesson of a sibling, share with the group.

2. Surely Moses wasn't the first "fine baby" to be born during the edict of killing the babies. From where do you think the courage of Moses' mother came?

3. Can you imagine the helplessness of watching your little brother float away down the river? What do you think was happening in Miriam as she watched?

4. Courage must have been a family trait. What do you admire about Miriam's interaction with Pharaoh's daughter?

5. Have you been tempted to think that the Lord is finished with you? What if the greatest years of being used by God are out in front of you? Would you look at the person next to you and ask them this question?

6. Based on our chapters so far, can you name one thing besides your agreement that could keep incredible feats for God from happening in your future?

7. God is everywhere, in the mundane and the extraordinary. Have you invited the Lord to be with you in every area of your life? What is your response to hearing that you can have God with you no matter your condition or circumstance?

8. The function of the prophet was to speak truth on God's behalf. What do you think Miriam might have been speaking to the people during those decades of slavery?

9. Miriam couldn't contain her worship after so many decades of slavery so she led in singing and dancing. Have you experience or witnessed freedom after an extended time of struggle, battle, or bondage? Tell of that experience.

10. Miriam's leadership took a dark turn—gossiping, judging Moses and even his family—and her consequences were severe. We are called to obey our spiritual leaders (Hebrews 13:17), not disparage them. What is your response to the command of honoring and obeying your leaders? Can you think of a time when you were called to honor and obey a leader and not just serve yourself?

11. What is one way that you can take a practical step of encouraging and honoring your pastor, teacher,

small-group leader, or mentor this week? Share with your group.

Prayer Focus

The living conditions for the Israelites got darker and darker as the decades went on, and the promises may have felt faint. At some level, they may have begun to accept that this was all there was and resign themselves to their fate of slavery. They didn't know that the Lord had a plan that started with a baby in a basket. We know of the plan of the baby in the cradle who purchased our freedom from bondage to our sin and the sin done to us, the brokenness we experience in nearly every place of life, addictions and family sin patterns. Will you go on record today and ask our Lord for a breakthrough in an area that has been long devastated?

Mighty God, you made the way on the cross for me to experience freedom in every area of my life. As Christ followers, the same power that raised Jesus from the dead lives in us. Please Lord; show me what it means to step into freedom from this particular area. I won't hold back my worship and gratitude.

Chapter 7
Israel's First Female Prime Minister

Chapter Summary

In this chapter we get to know Deborah, a woman who listened to the Lord and courageously led the way to help the Lord's people know what to do next.

Reflection/Discussion Questions

1. Read Psalm 85:8 as a group. Discuss the *who, what, when, where, why,* and *how* of the actions in this verse.

2. If our God is the same yesterday, today, and forever, then we can expect to hear! Take a minute as a group to pray for your ears to be open to anything the Lord might want to speak to you.

3. What struck you about Deborah as you read this chapter? What made Deborah a leader worth following?

4. In a vacuum of leadership, Deborah listened to the Lord and stepped in. Tell of someone in your life whose listening has made a way for you to experience the Lord more fully.

5. Deborah heard God calling the plays, and both on the battlefield and under the tree, she fought for those plays to come to pass. What were the results of her obedience?

6. What happened that day on the battlefield when the troops started marching?

7. Who fought for them in a seemingly impossible situation? Who really won the battle?

8. How do you think Deborah got to the point of being ready to be a judge of Israel? Did it happen under the tree or on the battlefield? If not, then where do you think that happened?

9. What personal practices or habits have aided you as you seek to listen to what our God has to say?

10. Have you sensed a vacuum of something around you where your gifts could be used for the kingdom of God? Where is that vacuum?

11. Would you be willing to get your hopes up that your life could have an influence that could last well beyond your years?

Prayer Focus

Deborah could have made a long and convincing list about why she wasn't the one to do what she did in her generation. She chose to listen and be obedient, not to be paralyzed by the reasons it should not be her. Is there a place you have been making a list as to why this next step should not be you? If the Lord is calling it, why would we think that God would not fight for us as in the days of Deborah?

Merciful God, please forgive me for making excuses when you have called me to listen and obey. All you need is my yes, and you can do mighty things through me in my generation. I want to be a person who will win battles for you. Help me remember your faithfulness as I step into the next part of my journey.

Chapter 8
The Perfect In-Laws

Chapter Summary

The focus of this chapter is Ruth, a widow who chose, for love, to take a chance on a people and a God that honored her risk in a beautiful way.

Reflection/Discussion Questions

1. Many would say the term *perfect in-laws* is an oxymoron. How is that term defined in this week's study?
2. The author said that it was "better to laugh about some matters than to rail hopelessly against them or to grow bitter in thinking of them." Some would say to laugh is a far more difficult task. What has been your inclination when life hasn't gone as you'd hoped?
3. When Naomi tried to send her daughters-in-law back to their home, she was also giving up her chance at redemption, because she was too old to be married again. Why do you think she was willing to do this?
4. Ruth's response to Naomi's insistence is poetic and beautifully loyal. Why was the bond so strong between them?
5. Naomi chose, in the midst of her pain, to blame God, as if she had been selected for misfortune. Tell of a time in your life when blaming God came easier than any other response.

6. Naomi was bitter and even changed her name to reflect her attitude. What if God would have let her settle in that place? Why do you think the Lord chose to bless her anyway?

7. I wonder if the biblical writer chuckled when he wrote of Ruth in Boaz's field, "as it happened." Share of a time in your life when Providence made a way for you.

8. Read Colossians 3:23 together. Paul was encouraging slaves in this verse to work for a different Master, a heavenly Master. How is it evident in Ruth's life that she was choosing to work and honor the Lord?

9. Boaz stepped in where Ruth was working and spoke kindly and warmly to her. He welcomed her to their land and their people. Who was one of the first people to speak kindly to you on behalf of the people of our God? What did he or she say?

10. Boaz encouraged Ruth for her actions and choices. Who is someone in your circle whom you could take time to encourage for their actions and choices? Take a moment this week to do so.

11. With the history of Israel and Moab, why do you think our God had a Moabite widow become part of the lineage of Jesus Christ?

Prayer Focus

Ruth seemed to understand, in the days before Christ, that the spiritual connection in our God could supersede racial, ethnic, and even blood ties. The generations that followed, including ours, have seemed to continue to strug-gle with this very thing. As Christ followers we are called to love all people and to share the good news with them. Where do you need to let God give you a sense and a heart for a group that has been difficult to love? Our Lord's heart transcends all bounds.

All-seeing and all-knowing God, only your love has the power to break down walls and barriers that have long since been standing. Lord, please help me see which people I have had a hard time loving and choose love for them. I am desperate for your heart and power, and I believe that you long to answer this kind of prayer.

Chapter 9
The Ladies' Chorus

Chapter Summary

This chapter gives us a glimpse of community at its finest—
a group of women who love, cry, celebrate, and support
Naomi on her journey toward restoration and wholeness.

Reflection/Discussion Questions

1. Our God knew every single name of each woman in
   the chorus and the role(s) that she would play along
   the journey: encouragements given, a pat on the shoulder, a hug, a listening ear, a word of hope. Do you
   believe the Lord orchestrates all of those things?

2. Have you ever had a sense of the Divine when you've
   come alongside another? What was that experience
   like?

3. After hearing of Naomi's circumstances in Moab, it is
   easy to stop with, "We knew no good would come of
   this move." Tell of a time when celebration and
   restoration came out of a "no good" situation.

4. We serve a God who works all things together for
   good! Take a minute and ask the Lord for a reinterpre-
   tation for a circumstance you may have written off as
   hopeless.

5. In these two chapters of Naomi and Ruth's story, what
   is the most moving piece to you personally?

6. These women saw Naomi for who she really was when she was choosing a path that made her less than pleasant to be around. Who is someone who didn't give up on you when you were in the pit? What was something important that he or she did during that season?

7. The Lord didn't provide children in Moab and was well aware that conception would happen in Israel. The pain was allowed because a greater good was coming. In fact, the only truly good person ever born came from this family. Who was Obed's grandson? Who came from his grandson's generations?

8. Every family has expectations and unwritten rules. What are some of those in your family?

9. What was your first response when you realized that the women of the village named Obed?

10. People who will laugh, cry, and celebrate with us are one of life's greatest gifts. Share a story of someone who does that with you.

11. What is one step of thanks or honor you can take for him or her this week?

Prayer Focus

In a world that moves as quickly as ours, we can miss when people around us are hurting. As grateful as we are for the choruses in our lives, we also get the privilege of being in the chorus for others. Whose chorus have you been chosen to be part of?

Almighty God, please open my eyes to the person or people around me who are in need of a chorus of love and support. Would you give me love, words, and direction to come alongside this dear one?

Chapter 10
The Woman Who Saved a King

Chapter Summary

This chapter shows how Abigail was a "clever and beautiful woman" whose quick action affected the history of her nation and its greatest king.

Reflection/Discussion Questions

1. David was surrounded by discontented men. Perhaps the reason he was able to lead them so well was that he was usually able to rise above their frustration. How did David get carried away in this chapter?

2. Was David justified in his response? What was your response to the meanness of Nabal?

3. How did Abigail step in and save the day?

4. Abigail reminded David that battles he had been called to fight were the Lord's and cautioned that this was not one of those battles. Is there a place you are getting caught up that is not supposed to be one of your battles? Who is someone you can talk to today to help you reevaluate the "battles" in your life?

5. Have you been around someone who can diffuse the most tense and painful of situations? Perhaps you are that someone. Tell of someone, like Abigail, who has been that voice to you or those you know and love.

6. The greatest leaders surround themselves with other great leaders and advisors. Who are your current advisors?

7. Great leaders also have a process of decision making established. What is your process for making decisions, big or small?

8. David had the wisdom to thank the Lord for rescuing him from his moment of idiocy. Tell of a time when the Lord was able to rescue you from idiocy of your own.

9. If you have yet to thank God for the help, take a moment to do so now. As a group, take some time to thank the Lord for intervention that was not coincidence.

10. Abigail reminded David of who he was and what he was made for. Who has been that voice for you and helped you get where you are today? Was it a parent, teacher, coach, friend?

11. David gave us a great example of humility and wisdom when at a perilous juncture. What crossroads do you find yourself faced with today? What is one step you can take this week toward the person you know you were made to be?

Prayer Focus

There are crossroad moments in every life, and looking back, it can be easier to see when we should have chosen differently. Can you think of such a moment? Are there amends to make? Do you need freedom? perspective?

wisdom? healing? forgiveness? Do you need to offer forgiveness?

Merciful and loving God, I come before you thankful for your mercies that are new every morning. You are faithful, God, and I ask that you would forgive me and help me receive your grace in this place. It is only possible through the cross of Jesus, and I come humbly. Please show me any next steps I need to take and give me the courage to take them.

Chapter 11
Counselor to Kings and Clergy

Chapter Summary

This chapter gives us a look at a woman whose decisions led her to the person she was meant to be, which gave her the influence to help a lost nation find their way back to the God they had forgotten.

Reflection/Discussion Questions

1. At twelve years old, Josiah started seeking God. How old were you when your seeking started?

2. Until Josiah heard the Scriptures, he did not know how lost he and his people were. In humility he understood and acknowledged how far gone they were. Do you remember where you were when you understood how in need you were of grace and forgiveness? Share of that moment.

3. Josiah went first with his full repentance and captured the heart of the Lord, and his nation followed. Have you ever thought about your repentance making a way for someone or many to follow? Who are you hoping will be in your wake?

4. David told his son Solomon about his God, "If you seek him, you will find him." Our God is the same yesterday, today, and forever. Generations later Josiah sought God and found him. And thousands of years

later, we can still find God. Tell of the time when you found our Lord.

5. The Lord saw Huldah's faithfulness and knew there would be a time when her ability to hear would be vital for a king in a desperate place. Who are the people around you who are in a desperate place? Are they at work? school? your neighborhood? the grocery store? sitting near you at church? Does one in particular come to mind?

6. In the midst of your seeking and sorting, who was the Huldah to help you find your way? How did she come alongside you? What did he or she help bring to light for you?

7. Josiah's faith led to action in the way of national reform. How has your faith led to action in your life?

8. We have God's word in our hands, it is not lost. And it is still meant to be a light for our path, to bring correction and discipline, healing, peace, and to guide us to joyous living. What steps are you taking to interact with the word? How are you allowing God's word to shape and transform you?

9. We live in a nation fighting to forget about Christianity. How do you remember in the midst of a culture much like Josiah's—where everything seems bent against it—that there is a God who really wants to speak to you?

10. The author said, "In the end, of course, we all decide for ourselves what kind of persons we will be." Have you decided who you will be? Share with the group who you long to be.

11. What is a step you can take this week that is in alignment with the "you" you want to be? If you need help sorting it out, find a Huldah who can help you hear.

Prayer Focus

If it is God's "gracious intention" that we can inquire of the Lord, what barriers stand in the way? Where do you need to repent and tear down what has been built in the way of your relationship with God? We do not have to settle in and forget that we were made to walk with God. Because of Jesus, we can approach the throne of grace with confidence, believing that we, too, can hear what our God has to say.

Dear Lord, you are a good steward and you steward your voice to those who will listen. I want to know you more, and I want to be a person who can be a Huldah in my sphere of influence. Please let your spirit bring me to a place of repentance and transform me into one who walks more and more closely with you for all of my days.

Chapter 12
Two Young Women of Courage

Chapter Summary

With this chapter, we finish the book with a glimpse of two courageous Jewish women with the commonality of audacious faith in a God they trusted to do mighty things.

Reflection/Discussion Questions

1. What is your favorite part of Esther's story?
2. What captured your attention about the servant girl?
3. What is your definition of courage?
4. Tell of a time when courage was demanded of you to take the next step.
5. Who is the most courageous person you have ever known? What was he or she like? Where did you see her courage lived out?
6. In our day, fewer and fewer people understand that there is a God who loves them and is fighting on their behalf for them to see and believe and come to a place of faith. What are the challenges we face to sharing that message?
7. Where is the area you need the most courage right now?
8. Take some time as a group and pray for courage for one another where you need it.
9. What is your courageous step this week? Share it with

the group so they can be praying and then set up a time to check in with someone in the group to let him or her know how it went.

10. The servant girl told Naaman where to go, and then the Lord made the way for Naaman to get to Elisha to be healed. Shane Stanford tells us, in his book of the same title, "You can't do everything . . . so do something!" In other words, no one is responsible for doing it all, but each of us is completely responsible for doing our part. Take a deep breath and tell somebody, "It's not all up to you!"

11. Would you allow your hopes to rise? The call on your life was designed for you to live out. Tell our God that there does not need to be a search for a replacement. You can do this together!

Prayer Focus

While we most likely will not find ourselves in a place of Esther or this servant girl, our opportunities to exercise courage and boldness will be plentiful if we choose to embrace the calling of Jesus to share the good news with all people. This is not an easy endeavor, and it is a command from our God. What if we cared enough for those around us who do not yet know our God that we would risk ourselves on their behalf? Surely another will be employed if we say no, but what if we, like the apostles, choose not to keep silent? We could change the very world!

Lord God, your desire is that all men and women would know you. You sent your son for the whole world. Will you give me courage in the midst of rejection, fear, misunderstanding, and a generally full life? Will you help me be one who, without regard for myself, will see health and joy come into the lives of many who get to know you? You created me, in my place, for such a time as this. Please, Lord, give me faith to trust and act in every place you will let me.

Notes

1. The Ultimate First Lady

1. Kilian McDonnell, *Yahweh's Other Shoe* (Collegeville, Minn.: Saint John's University Press, 2006), 4.
2. Leon R. Kass, *The Beginning of Wisdom* (Chicago: University of Chicago Press, 2003), 101.
3. McDonnell, *Yahweh's*, 5.
4. Robert Alter, *The Five Books of Moses* (New York: W. W. Norton, 2004), 22.
5. Ibid., 29.
6. Kass, *Beginning*, 149.

2. A Woman Who Married Trouble

1. *Ancient Christian Commentary on Scripture, Genesis 1-11*, ed. Andrew Louth (Downers Grove, Ill.: InterVarsity Press, 2001), 110.
2. Leon R. Kass, *The Beginning of Wisdom* (Chicago: University of Chicago Press, 2003), 142.
3. Chad Walsh, ed., *The Honey and the Gall* (New York: Macmillan, 1967), 142]
4. Louth, *Ancient Christian Commentary*, 108.

3. The Compleat Woman

1. Leon R. Kass, *The Beginning of Wisdom* (Chicago: University of Chicago Press, 2003), 250.

4. A Mother Who Played Favorites

1. Maurice Samuel, *Certain People of the Book* (New York: Alfred A. Knopf, 1955), 149.
2. Ibid., 163.

3. Ibid., 168, 169.
4. Leon R. Kass, *The Beginning of Wisdom* (Chicago: University of Illinois Press, 2003), 401.

5. They May Have Been Twins—but Not Identical

1. Robert Alter, *The Five Books of Moses* (New York: W. W. Norton, 2004), 154.
2. Leon R. Kass, *The Beginning of Wisdom* (Chicago: University of Chicago Press, 2003), 428.

7. Israel's First Female Prime Minister

1. William Wordsworth, *The Complete Poetical Works* (London: Macmillan, 1888); Bartleby.com, 1999. www.bartleby.com/145.

10. The Woman Who Saved a King

1. www.qotd.com.

12. Two Young Women of Courage

1. Walter M. Abbott, Arthur Gilbert, Rolfe Lanier Hunt, J. Carter Swaim, *The Bible Reader* (London: Geoffrey Chapman Ltd., 1969), 307.